Achieving TABE® Success
in Mathematics

Level M

McGraw Hill Education

Cover photo: © Pixtal/SuperStock

MHEonline.com

Send all inquiries to:
McGraw-Hill Education
8787 Orion Place
Columbus, OH 43240

ISBN: 978-0-07-704468-8
MHID: 0-07-704468-1

Printed in the United States of America.

16 17 18 19 20 QVS 20 19 18 17 16 15

Table of Contents

To the Learner

In our global technological society, mathematics skills are more important than ever. The pages in *Achieving TABE Success in Math, Level M* provide instruction to help you increase your understanding of many basic mathematical ideas. These pages also include problems that allow you to practice and strengthen that understanding.

Start by taking the pretest on pages 1–6. Then use the answer key on page 7 to check your answers. There is an evaluation chart on page 7 that tells you which skill area is addressed by each problem in the pretest. This chart helps you identify your areas of strength and determine skill areas that need greater attention.

The main part of the book is organized into sections by skill area: The Number System, Addition, Subtraction, Multiplication, Division, Fractions, Decimals, Data Analysis, Algebra, Measurement, and Geometry. As you complete each page, check your answers using the answer key at the back of the book. Rework problems that you miss, and be sure to check with your instructor if you find you are having difficulty. At the end of each section you will find a Skills Checkup that serves as a quiz for that section. Answers for the Skills Checkup are included in the answer key at the back of the book.

The posttest on pages 159–167 will measure your overall progress and determine whether you have mastered the skills you need to move to the next level. By successfully completing *Achieving TABE Success in Math, Level M*, you will have a strong foundation on which to continue building your skills in mathematics.

Correlation Chart

Correlations Between Contemporary's Instructional Materials and TABE® Math Computation and Applied Math

Test 2 Mathematics Computation

Subskill	TABE® Form 9	TABE® Form 10	TABE® Survey 9	TABE® Survey 10	Practice and Instruction Pages			
					Achieving TABE Success in Mathematics, Level M	Number Power *	Number Sense **	Math Exercises ***
Addition of Whole Numbers								
no regrouping: up to 3 digits	7	——	1, 8	3, 5	15–18	1: 15–18	1: 17–25	1: 5, 6
no regrouping: column to 3 digits	1, 2, 9	3, 5	——	——	15–18	1: 15–18	1: 17–25	
regrouping: up to 3 digits	3, 5	——	3, 5	——	1: 19–24	1: 26–29	1: 7	
regrouping: column to 3 digits	——	1, 7	——	1	19–20	1: 19–24	1: 26–29	
regrouping: up to 4 digits	——	10	——	7	19–20	1: 31–32	1: 29–32	
Subtraction of Whole Numbers								
no regrouping: from 2 or 3 digits	4, 11, 17	2, 4	2, 7	2	26–28	1: 35–37	1: 39–44	1: 10, 11
no regrouping: from 4 digits	——	11	——	6	28	1: 38		
regrouping: from 2 or 3 digits	14, 25	8, 9, 13	9	10	29–30	1: 39–41	1: 45–54	1: 12, 13
regrouping: from 4 digits	27	26	16	16	29–30	1: 41–48	1: 55–61	
Multiplication of Whole Numbers								
no regrouping: by 1 digit	8, 12	12	4	9	36–38	1: 62–65	2: 7–15	1: 16
no regrouping: by 2+ by 1 digits	15, 18	16, 24, 27	10, 12	11, 14	41–42	1: 66–70	2: 19	1: 17
regrouping: by 1 digit	6, 10	6	6	4	39	1: 71–72	2: 16–18	1: 18–20
regrouping: by 2+ digits	26	18, 30	17	18	43	1: 72–75	2: 20–24	1: 18–20

Subskill	TABE® Form 9	TABE® Form 10	TABE® Survey 9	TABE® Survey 10	Practice and Instruction Pages			
					Achieving TABE Success in Mathematics, Level M	*Number Power ****	*Number Sense *****	*Math Exercises *******
Division of Whole Numbers								
no remainder: by 1 digit	20, 22, 28	19, 22	14, 18	13	48–52	1: 90–98	2: 30–35,	1: 22, 23 42–43
no remainder: by 2+ digits	39	——	24	——	58	1: 100–106	2: 44, 53–55	
remainder: by 1 digit	32, 35	25, 29, 40	22	15, 20, 24	53–57		2: 36–41	1: 24, 25
remainder: by 2+ digits	——	38	——	——	58	1: 109–110	2: 45, 53–55	1: 26
Decimals								
addition	16, 21, 24	17, 23, 32	11, 15	12, 19	89	2: 73	3: 26–44	2: 12, 13
subtraction	13, 36	15, 20	13	8	90	2: 75	3: 45–67	2: 14, 15
multiplication	30, 34	14, 34	20	22	91	2: 79–82	4: 7–31	2: 17, 18, 19
Fractions								
addition	31, 33, 37, 40	33, 35, 36, 39	21, 25	21, 23	71	2: 22–28	5: 7–39	3: 7–11
subtraction	19, 23, 29, 38	21, 28, 31, 37	19, 23	17, 25	71	2: 31–36	5: 39–67	3: 13–17

Test 3 Applied Mathematics

Number and Number Operations								
read, recognize numbers	——	2	——	——	10, 64, 85–86	2: 64–65	1: 10–12	2: 3–5, 7
money	23	10	——	10	31		3: 36–44, 69–71 4: 66–73	1: 4, 8, 14, 20, 23
operations sense	31	36, 48	17	23	44–59			4: 5–7
compare, order	6	4	——	——	11, 69, 88	2: 70	1: 14–16 6: 21–26, 35–40	2: 6
place value	22	30	——	19	8–9, 84	1: 6–10 2: 62–63	1: 7–11 3: 7–25	2: 4, 5, 10–11
fractional part	39	45	21		63	2: 11–20	6: 7–20	3: 3–6
operation properties	42	——	——	——	15, 26, 36, 48, 114–115			

Subskill	TABE® Form 9	TABE® Form 10	TABE® Survey 9	TABE® Survey 10	Practice and Instruction Pages			
					Achieving TABE Success in Mathematics, Level M	*Number Power **	*Number Sense ***	*Math Exercises ****
equivalent forms	10, 48	49	1	24	9, 65, 67–68, 74–81, 86–87	2: 68–69	6: 27–34 7: 7–33	3: 6
number line	8	38	13	——	131–134	3: 11–17		6: 3
factors, multiples, divisibility	1	6	——	1	40, 60, 70			
Computation in Context								
whole numbers	5, 16, 30	12, 39	——	——	22, 32, 44, 59	1: 27–30, 52–56, 79–83, 111–116 6: 18–39, 61–88	1: 33–38, 63–74 2: 57–74	1: 9, 15, 21, 27, 29
decimals	——	9, 46	——	6	93	2: 74, 77, 84–85 6: 40–51	3: 36–44, 57–74 4: 24–31, 51–74	2: 16, 20
fractions	38	35	20	18	77	2: 30, 37–38, 6: 52–55	5: 32–38, 59–74	3: 12, 18
Estimation								
estimation	14, 19, 28	5, 43	9, 15	21	31–32, 43, 55, 74	1: 25–26, 50–51, 76–78, 107–108 2: 44	2: 46–52 4: 8–9	2: 8–9
rounding	21	3	——	——	12, 21, 31, 92	1: 11–12, 25–26, 50–51, 76–78, 107–108 2: 44, 71–72	2: 50	1: 3, 4 2: 10–11
reasonableness of answer	33	20	——	9	21, 59			
Measurement								
use ruler	37	42	19	20	131–133	2: 134–135 9: 12–13		7: 4, 5
appropriate unit	35	44	——	4	124–125			7: 14–21
time	27	19	——	8	137–140	9: 128–145		
temperature	——	37	——	——	134	9: 74–83 3: 180–181	3: 68	7: 25–26

Subskill	TABE® Form 9	TABE® Form 10	TABE® Survey 9	TABE® Survey 10	Practice and Instruction Pages			
					Achieving TABE Success in Mathematics, Level M	Number Power *	Number Sense **	Math Exercises ***
length, distance	34, 44	——	22	——	125–127	2: 147–149 4: 82–85 9: 28–37	1: 71 6: 64–67	7: 6–11
perimeter	45	18, 24	23	7	135	1: 135–136 2: 136–137 4: 88–89		5: 20
Geometry and Spatial Sense								
symmetry	——	23	——	——	151			
congruence, similarity	3, 9	22, 29	3	——	152–153	4: 52–61 14–15		5: 8–11,
solid figure	17	17	12	2	154	4: 125–142		5: 26, 27
visualization, spatial reasoning	——	1	——	——	150, 155	4: 176–177, 182–183		
parallel, perpendicular	24, 25	50	——	25	145	4: 18–19, 30–33		5: 8–9
triangles	36	——	14	——	148	4: 38–69		5: 10–11, 14–15, 18–19, 24
Data Analysis								
bar, line, and circle graph	40	11, 25, 26	——	11, 22	102–106	5: 12–67		8: 12–17
table, chart, diagram	4, 11, 26	——	4, 6	——	96–99	1: 159–161		8: 3–5
conclusions from data	7, 12, 41	13, 28	5, 7	——	97, 104–106	5: 12–67, 77–95		8: 18–19
appropriate data display	——	33	——	16				
Statistics and Probability								
probability	49, 50	14, 15	24, 25	——	107			8: 20–26
statistics	15, 43	27, 31	10	13, 14	100–101	5: 166–181		
Patterns, Functions, Algebra								
number pattern	2	21	2	——	112			
geometric pattern	——	34	——	17	110–111			

Subskill	TABE® Form 9	TABE® Form 10	TABE® Survey 9	TABE® Survey 10	Practice and Instruction Pages			
					Achieving TABE Success in Mathematics, Level M	*Number Power* *	*Number Sense* **	*Math Exercises* ***
variable, expression, equation	20	16, 40	11	3	117–121	3: 38–49, 52–63, 68–80		4: 14–16 6: 8–11, 14–23
function	46, 47	47	——	22	116			
Problem Solving and Reasoning								
solve problem	13, 32	7	8, 18	——	22–23, 32–33, 59, 77, 93	6: 10–17		4: 3, 10–13
identify missing/ extra information	29	32	16	15	23, 33, 45	6: 14–17		4: 4, 18–19
model problem situation, solution	18	8, 41	——	5	60, 93	6: 34–36, 48–49, 54, 72–76		

* Number Power 1: Addition, Subtraction, Multiplication, Division; 2: Fractions, Decimals, Percents; 3: Algebra; 4: Geometry; 5: Graphs, Tables, Schedules, Maps; 6: Word Problems; 9: Measurement

** Number Sense 1: Whole Numbers, Addition & Subtraction; 2: Whole Numbers, Multiplication & Division; 3: Decimals, Addition & Subtraction; 4: Decimals, Multiplication & Division; 5: Fractions, Addition & Subtraction; 6: Fractions, The Meaning of Fractions; 7: Ratio & Proportion

*** Math Exercises 1: Whole Numbers and Money; 2: Decimals; 3: Fractions; 4: Problem Solving & Applications; 5: Geometry; 6: Pre-Algebra; 7: Measurement; 8: Data Analysis & Probability

TABE® Forms 9 and 10 are published by CTB/McGraw-Hill.
TABE is a registered trademark of The McGraw-Hill Companies.

Skills Inventory Pretest

Part A: Computation

Circle the letter for the correct answer to each problem.

1. $10 \times 8 =$
   - A 80
   - B 18
   - C 88
   - D 108
   - E None of these

2.
   $$\begin{array}{r} 3,016 \\ + \ 2,963 \end{array}$$
   - F 5,978
   - G 6,979
   - H 5,989
   - J 5,979
   - K None of these

3.
   $$\begin{array}{r} 114 \\ - \ \ 95 \end{array}$$
   - A 39
   - B 18
   - C 19
   - D 21
   - E None of these

4.
   $$\begin{array}{r} 67 \\ \times \ \ 12 \end{array}$$
   - F 704
   - G 794
   - H 201
   - J 804
   - K None of these

5. $7 \div 5 =$
   - A 2
   - B 1
   - C 1 R2
   - D 2 R1
   - E None of these

6. $72 \div 3 =$
   - F 14
   - G 20 R2
   - H 24
   - J 23
   - K None of these

7. $446 + 282 =$
   - A 628
   - B 728
   - C 718
   - D 638
   - E None of these

8. $\dfrac{12}{15} - \dfrac{3}{15} =$
   - F $\dfrac{3}{5}$ H 1
   - G 9   J $2\dfrac{2}{3}$
   - K None of these

9. $23.05 + 7.9 =$
   - A 30.95
   - B 30.14
   - C 102.05
   - D 23.94
   - E None of these

10. $34 \times 0.5 =$
    - F 120
    - G 12.0
    - H 1.2
    - J 0.12
    - K None of these

11. $68.1 - 15.07 =$
    - A 53.17
    - B 53.03
    - C 83.17
    - D 53.13
    - E None of these

12.

$100 \times 0.435 =$

- F 43.5
- G 435
- H 0.00435
- J 4.35
- K None of these

13.

$1250 - 129 =$

- A 1,111
- B 1,139
- C 1,121
- D 1,131
- E None of these

14.

$\dfrac{1}{2}$

$+ \dfrac{3}{4}$

- F $\dfrac{2}{3}$
- G $1\dfrac{1}{4}$
- H $1\dfrac{1}{2}$
- J 1
- K None of these

15.

$20\overline{)640}$

- A 320
- B 150
- C 45
- D 32
- E None of these

16.

427
1,650
+ 4,803

- F 6,870
- G 6,887
- H 6,880
- J 6,803
- K None of these

17.

$23\overline{)58}$

- A 2
- B 2 R5
- C 1 R35
- D 2 R12
- E None of these

18.

$12\dfrac{1}{2}$

$- 5\dfrac{3}{8}$

- F $7\dfrac{1}{16}$
- G $7\dfrac{1}{4}$
- H $7\dfrac{2}{5}$
- J $7\dfrac{1}{8}$
- K None of these

19.

$18\overline{)414}$

- A 27
- B 32
- C 28
- D 20 R10
- E None of these

20.

$\dfrac{1}{5} + \dfrac{3}{5} + \dfrac{1}{5} =$

- F $1\dfrac{1}{5}$
- G $\dfrac{5}{15}$
- H 1
- J $\dfrac{3}{10}$
- K None of these

Part B: Applied Mathematics

Circle the letter for the correct answer to each problem.

1. Which of these units of measure is the most appropriate for measuring the height of a desk?

   A centimeters
   B millimeters
   C kilometers
   D meters

2. What sign goes in the box to make the number sentence true?

   $$12 \ \square \ 12 = 1$$

   F $\times$
   G $\div$
   H $-$
   J $+$

3. What number is missing from this number sequence?

   $$100, 80, \underline{\hspace{1cm}}, 40, 20$$

   A 5
   B 25
   C 60
   D 40

4. What time will the clock show in 20 minutes?

   F 3:20
   G 3:25
   H 3:45
   J 3:35

Keiko has weighed her baby every month for the last 6 months. This table shows her records. Study the table. Then do Numbers 5–7.

Age	Weight
2 days	6 pounds 1 ounce
1 month	6 pounds 9 ounces
2 months	7 pounds 1 ounce
3 months	7 pounds 8 ounces
4 months	8 pounds 1 ounce
5 months	8 pounds 9 ounces

5. How much weight did the baby gain during this time?

   A 8 pounds 9 ounces
   B 2 pounds 11 ounces
   C 2 pounds 8 ounces
   D 2 pounds 9 ounces

6. The baby has gained weight at a pretty steady rate. About how much did the baby gain each month?

   F 8 ounces
   G 1 pound
   H 2 ounces
   J 19 ounces

7. How much did the baby weigh at 3 months of age?

   A $7\frac{1}{3}$ pounds

   B $7\frac{1}{4}$ pounds

   C $7\frac{1}{2}$ pounds

   D $7\frac{4}{5}$ pounds

8. In 17,892, what does the 7 mean?

    F 70   **H** 7,000

    G 700   **J** 70,000

9. If the same number is used in both boxes, which of these statements would be true?

    A If $7 - \square = 3$, then $3 - \square = 7$.

    B If $13 - \square = 8$, then $13 + 8 = \square$.

    C If $7 + \square = 12$, then $12 \div \square = 7$.

    D If $3 \times \square = 15$, then $15 \div \square = 3$.

10. Lana is making ice for her party. She can only freeze 24 cubes at a time. If she makes 4 batches of ice cubes, how many cubes will she have?

    F 28   **H** 86

    G 64   **J** 96

11. Alli spent $26.78 for a shirt, $41.15 for some pants, and $72.59 for a pair of shoes. Which number sentence should he use to estimate to the nearest dollar how much he spent?

    A $26 + $41 + $72 = \square$

    B $27 + $41 + $73 = \square$

    C $26 + $41 + $73 = \square$

    D $27 + $41 + $72 = \square$

12. Tia tossed a number cube labeled with the numbers 1 through 6. What are the chances she tossed a number greater than one?

    F likely

    G not likely

    H impossible

    J certain

13. Don had $22 in his wallet. He withdrew another $40 from an ATM machine. Then he spent $12 for lunch. How much cash is left in his wallet?

    A $60   **C** $28

    B $10   **D** $50

This graph appeared in a newspaper article on teenage pregnancy. Study the graph. Then use it to do Numbers 14–16.

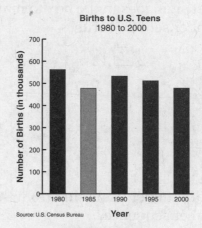

Births to U.S. Teens 1980 to 2000

Source: U.S. Census Bureau   **Year**

14. In which 2 years did approximately the same number of teens give birth?

    F 1980 and 1995

    G 1985 and 2000

    H 1990 and 2000

    J No two years had the same number.

15. Which number represents an approximate average of the number of teens giving birth during the period shown?

    A 600,000   **C** 400,000

    B 500,000   **D** 300,000

16. Based on the data in this graph, which is the best estimate of the number of U.S. teens that will give birth in 2005?

    F more than 600,000

    G between 550,000 and 650,000

    H between 450,000 and 550,000

    J fewer than 400,000

This table shows travel times as a commuter train makes four stops after our station. Use the table to answer Numbers 29–31.

Travel Times from Central Station

Stop	Travel Time
Grant Street	12 minutes
Hohoken Street	16 minutes
Bentley Avenue	22 minutes
City Zoo	31 minutes

17. You want to travel from Central Station to the zoo and back. How much time would you spend on the train?

    A 31 minutes

    B 44 minutes

    C 62 minutes

    D $16\frac{1}{2}$ minutes

18. The travel time to Bentley Avenue is about $\frac{1}{3}$ of an hour. That is between which two amounts of time?

    F $\frac{1}{4}$ and $\frac{1}{2}$ of an hour

    G $\frac{1}{2}$ and $\frac{3}{4}$ of an hour

    H $\frac{3}{4}$ and $\frac{2}{3}$ of an hour

    J $\frac{1}{6}$ and $\frac{1}{5}$ of an hour

19. Which of these is the best estimate of the travel time from Bentley Avenue to the City Zoo?

    A   5 minutes
    B 10 minutes
    C 15 minutes
    D 20 minutes

20. What is the temperature shown on this thermometer?

    F 90°F
    G 91°F
    H 92°F
    J 94°F

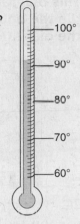

21. Hector must pay $102.50 in taxes. Which of the following amounts should he put on his check to the government?

    A one hundred twenty and $\frac{5}{100}$

    B one hundred two and $\frac{50}{100}$

    C one thousand two and $\frac{50}{100}$

    D one hundred two and $\frac{5}{100}$

22. Which of these numbers is a common factor of 9 and 24?

    F 2
    G 3
    H 6
    J 9

23. Which of the following decimals, rounded to the nearest whole number, is 35?

    A 35.96
    B 34.94
    C 34.14
    D 35.67

This diagram shows how an artist plans to tile the bottom of a swimming pool. Study the diagram. Then do Numbers 24 and 25.

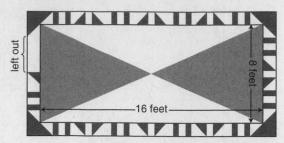

24. A section of the pool border is missing on the left side. Which of the figures below shows the section that is missing?

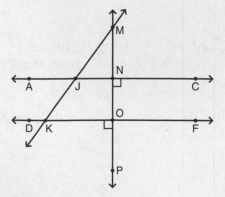

F
H
G
J

25. What is the perimeter of the inside of the border?

A 24 feet   C 48 feet
B 128 feet   D 64 feet

26. What is the best way to describe the relationship between line *AC* and line *DF*?

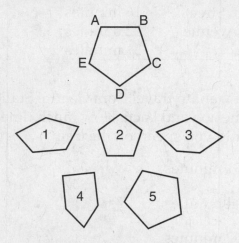

F perpendicular
G parallel
H intersecting
J adjoining

27. What is the value of the expression $7 + (6 \times y)$ if $y = 4$?

A 17   C 31
B 168   D 66

28. Which figures are similar to figure *ABCDE*?

F 1 and 3   H 2 and 4
G 1, 3 and 4   J 2 and 5

29. Which group of numbers is in order from least to greatest?

A 23.05; 23.2; 23.14; 23.003
B 23.2; 23.05; 23.14; 23.003
C 23.2; 23.003; 23.05; 23.14
D 23.003; 23.05; 23.14; 23.2

30. What is the correct value for Point *P* on the number line?

F $1\dfrac{1}{5}$

G $3\dfrac{3}{10}$

H $2\dfrac{3}{4}$

J $1\dfrac{1}{4}$

Skills Inventory Pretest Evaluation

Use the answer keys to check your pretest. The evaluation charts match each problem in the pretest to a skill area. The charts will refer you to pages in this book that can provide information and practice to help you with problems you missed.

Answer Key—Part A: Computation

1.	A	11.	B
2.	J	12.	F
3.	C	13.	C
4.	J	14.	G
5.	C	15.	D
6.	H	16.	H
7.	B	17.	D
8.	F	18.	J
9.	A	19.	E
10.	K	20.	H

Evaluation Chart—Part A: Computation

Problem Number	Skill Area	Text Pages
2, 7, 16	Addition of Whole Numbers	15–21
3, 13	Subtraction of Whole Numbers	26–30
1, 4	Multiplication of Whole Numbers	36–42
5, 6, 15, 17, 19	Division of Whole Numbers	48–58
8, 14, 18, 20	Fractions	63–80, 86
9, 10, 11, 12	Decimals	75–76, 84–93

Answer Key—Part B: Applied Mathematics

1.	A	16.	H
2.	G	17.	C
3.	C	18.	F
4.	J	19.	B
5.	C	20.	H
6.	F	21.	B
7.	C	22.	G
8.	H	23.	B
9.	D	24.	F
10.	J	25.	C
11.	B	26.	G
12.	F	27.	C
13.	D	28.	J
14.	G	29.	D
15.	B	30.	J

Evaluation Chart—Part B: Applied Mathematics

Problem Number	Skill Area	Text Pages
2, 8, 9, 18, 21, 22, 29, 30	Number and Number Operations	8–12, 15–20, 26–30, 36–42, 48–54, 56–58, 120
10, 13	Computation in Context	44–45, 59–60, 93, 139
6, 11, 19, 23	Estimation	12, 21, 31–32, 43, 55, 65, 74, 92
1, 4, 20, 25	Measurement	124–140
26, 28	Geometry and Spatial Sense	110, 143–154
7, 14, 16	Data Analysis	98–99, 102–106
12, 15	Statistics and Probability	100–101, 107
3, 24, 27	Patterns, Functions, Algebra	110–121
5, 17	Problem Solving and Reasoning	22–23, 32–33, 44–45, 59–60, 93, 139, 155

The Number System

Reviewing Place Value

To read, write, and work with numbers, you need to understand our **place-value system**. You can write a number to represent any amount, no matter how large or how small, using these ten symbols or **digits**: 0, 1, 2, 3, 4, 5, 6, 7, 8, and 9. The value of the digit depends on its place in the number.

The place-value chart at right shows how we organize whole numbers in "families" called *ones, thousands, millions, billions,* and so on.

billions	hundred millions	ten millions	millions	hundred thousands	ten thousands	thousands	hundreds	tens	ones
···			millions			thousands		ones	···
				7	3	5	8	1	
						1	5	8	

- Each family has three members: ones, tens, and hundreds. Commas are used to separate the families. The commas help us to read numbers more easily.

- The value of a digit is determined by its place in the number.
  In 73,581, the digit 5 is in the hundreds place.
  $5 \times 100 = 500$, so the 5 has a value of 500.

  In 158, the digit 5 is in the tens place.
  $5 \times 10 = 50$, so the 5 has a value of 50.

PRACTICE

Identify the place and the value of the 4 in each number.

1. 4,853

    thousands; 4,000

2. 3,490

3. 24,680

4. 641,935

5. 249

6. 42,062

7. 53,984

8. 33,547

9. 40,157,098

10. 418,761

11. 4,605,739

12. 403,199,513

Writing Whole Numbers in Expanded Form

You can show the value of each digit in a number by writing the number in **expanded form**.

Example   35,572 = 3 ten thousands + 5 thousands + 5 hundreds + 7 tens + 2 ones
              = 30,000 + 5,000 + 500 + 70 + 2

If the digit in a place is 0, you do not need to include that place in the expanded form.

Example   50,740 = 5 ten thousands + 0 thousands + 7 hundreds + 4 tens + 0 ones
              = 50,000 + 700 + 40

Note: In expanded form you only need to write the value of the nonzero digits.

PRACTICE

Write each standard numeral in expanded form. Be sure to include the correct number of zeros to show the value of each digit.

1. 13,256   _____

2. 481,504   _____

3. 6,013   _____

4. 907,334   _____

To write the standard numeral from the expanded form, make sure each digit is written in the correct place. Fill in places not shown with zeros.

Example   60,000 + 7,000 + 400 + 8 = 60 thousands + 7 thousands + 4 hundreds + 8 ones
              standard numeral = 67,408

PRACTICE

Write the standard numeral.

5. 10,000 + 400 + 50 + 7 =   _____

6. 200,000 + 8,000 + 500 + 40 + 3 =   _____

7. 1,000,000 + 7,000 + 90 + 6 =   _____

8. 40,000 + 3,000 + 600 + 70 =   _____

Reading and Writing Whole Numbers

Reading numbers is easy. You can use expanded form to help you.

Examples $157 = 100 + 50 + 7 =$ one hundred fifty-seven
$408 = 400 + 8 =$ four hundred eight

To read larger numbers, start at the left and work to the right. Work with one family at a time. Read the three digits in the family just as you would read numbers in the ones family, but then say the family name. Remember, commas separate the families.

Examples $27,104 =$ twenty-seven thousand, one hundred four
$190,003 =$ one hundred ninety thousand, three
$5,472,900 =$ five million, four hundred seventy-two thousand, nine hundred

PRACTICE

Circle the letter of the words that match the number.

1. 700,590
   A seven thousand, fifty-nine
   B seven hundred thousand fifty-nine
   C seven hundred thousand, five hundred ninety

2. 38,930
   F thirty-eight thousand, ninety-three
   G three hundred eight thousand, ninety-three
   H thirty-eight thousand, nine hundred thirty

3. 109,099
   A one hundred nine thousand, ninety-nine
   B nineteen thousand, ninety-nine
   C one hundred thousand, nine hundred nine

4. 68,030
   F sixty-eight, thirty
   G sixty-eight thousand, thirty
   H sixty-eight thousand, three

5. 2,800,802
   A two million, eighty thousand, eight hundred two
   B two million, eight thousand, eight hundred two
   C two million, eight hundred thousand, eight hundred two

6. 420,000
   F forty-two thousand
   G four hundred twenty thousand
   H four hundred two thousand

Write the standard numeral. Write a zero to fill a place that is not named.

7. six thousand, twelve

   _____

8. eight hundred six thousand, one hundred eighty-three

   _____

9. one hundred forty thousand, sixty-five

   _____

10. seventeen million, seventeen thousand, seventy

   _____

Comparing Whole Numbers

To compare whole numbers, check the number of places.

- If the number of digits **is not the same**, the number that has more digits is greater.

Example Compare 2,003 and 998.

      2,003 has four digits (thousands)
       998 has three digits (hundreds)
      2,003 is greater than 998.

- If the number of digits **is the same**, compare the digits in each place. Start at the left and work to the right.

Example Compare 4,572 and 4,752.

      4,572 Check the thousands place. The thousands digit is 4 in both numbers.
      4,752 Check the hundreds place. Seven hundreds are greater than five hundreds.
      4,752 is greater than 4,572.

PRACTICE

Circle the greater number in each pair.

1. 2,842   546

2. 193   20

3. 21,403   899

4. 89   98

5. 876   413

6. 12,075   12,705

Circle the greatest number in each set.

7. 16,000   8,000   20,000

8. 9   51   13

9. 11,000   719   3,230

10. 29   98   160

11. 13   9   5

12. 1,720   1,702   957

Arrange these numbers from least to greatest.

13. 97, 115, 146, 52

_____

14. 103, 95, 17, 9

_____

15. 178, 517, 203, 695, 961

_____

Arrange these digits to make the least number possible.

16. 2, 1, 7   _____

17. 8, 7, 6   _____

Arrange these digits to make the greatest number possible.

18. 9, 2, 3   _____

19. 4, 8, 2, 5   _____

Rounding Whole Numbers

We often use **rounded** numbers to estimate an amount. An **estimate** is a number that is close to the actual or exact amount. For example, you might say you drove about 500 miles, but the exact number was 493 miles.

You can round numbers to different place values. The rounding method shown below for rounding to the nearest ten and nearest hundred can be extended to greater place values.

Rounding to the Nearest Ten
- Identify the digit in the tens place. The tens digit either stays the same *or* it becomes greater by one. What happens depends on the ones digit.
- Look at the digit in the ones place. If the ones digit is 4 or less, the tens digit stays the same. If the ones digit is 5 or greater, increase the tens digit by one.
- Change the ones digit to 0.

Examples
Round 485 to the nearest ten.

485   The ones digit is 5.
485 rounds to 490.

Round 94 to the nearest ten.

94   The ones digit is less than 5.
94 rounds to 90.

PRACTICE

Round each number to the nearest ten.

1. 382 _____ 2. 1,448 _____ 3. 43 _____ 4. 8 _____

Rounding to the Nearest Hundred
- Identify the digit in the hundreds place. The hundreds digit stays the same *or* it becomes greater by one. What happens depends on the tens digit.
- Look at the digit in the tens place. If the tens digit is 4 or less, the hundreds digit stays the same. If the tens digit is 5 or greater, increase the hundreds digit by one.
- Change both the tens digit and the ones digit to 0.

Examples
Round 435 to the nearest hundred.

435   The tens digit is less than 5.
435 rounds to 400.

Round 94 to the nearest hundred.

94   The tens digit is greater than 5.
94 rounds to 100.

PRACTICE

Round each number to the nearest hundred.

5. 290 _____ 6. 89 _____ 7. 457 _____ 8. 12,075 _____

Number System Skills Checkup

Circle the letter for the correct answer to each question.

1. What is the value of the digit 6 in the number 26,503?

   A   60
   B   600
   C   6,000
   D 60,000
   E None of these

2. Which of the following numbers is *greater* than 3,645?

   F 2,759
   G 3,367
   H 3,731
   J 3,639
   K None of these

3. Which of these numbers is 819 rounded to the nearest ten?

   A 900
   B 800
   C 810
   D 820
   E None of these

4. Which of these has the same value as 6,000 + 500 + 2?

   F   652
   G 6,502
   H 6,520
   J 6,052
   K None of these

Use the information below to answer Questions 5–7.

Mr. and Mrs. Suarez just opened an ice cream shop. This list shows how many people visited the shop each of the first four days.

Friday	109
Saturday	167
Sunday	182
Monday	98

5. On which day did the shop have the greatest number of customers?

   A Friday
   B Saturday
   C Sunday
   D Monday

6. On which days were there fewer than 150 customers?

   F Friday and Saturday
   G Saturday and Sunday
   H Sunday and Monday
   J Friday and Monday

7. Mrs. Suarez decided to estimate the total number of customers by rounding each number to the nearest ten. Which set of numbers shows the correct estimates?

   A 100, 200, 100, 100
   B 180, 160, 100, 90
   C 180, 170, 100, 100
   D 110, 170, 180, 100

Number System Skills Checkup (continued)

8. You hear that the new city manager will earn one hundred twenty thousand dollars a year. Which of these numbers shows one hundred twenty thousand dollars?

   F $ 120,000
   G $ 12,000
   H $ 102,000
   J $1,020,000
   K None of these

9. In which number is the digit in the ten thousands place greater than the digit in the tens place?

   A 532,364
   B 752,684
   C 142,334
   D 185,394
   E None of these

10. In which pair will both numbers round to 500?

    F 435 and 535
    G 480 and 567
    H 475 and 575
    J 450 and 529
    K None of these

11. Which of these numbers is equal to eighty thousand?

    A 80,000
    B 18,000
    C 800,000
    D 180,000
    E None of these

12. Which group of numbers is arranged from greatest to least?

    F 13,270; 12,370; 9,736; 9,734
    G 9,734; 9,736; 13,270; 12,370
    H 13,270; 9,734; 9,736; 12,370
    J 12,370; 13,270; 9,734; 9,736

13. The XYZ Company figured that their total sales last year amounted to $19,560,000. What is this amount in words?

    A nineteen million, five hundred sixty dollars
    B nineteen billion, five hundred sixty million dollars
    C nineteen million, five hundred six thousand dollars
    D nineteen million, five hundred sixty thousand dollars

14. In which number is the value of the digit in the ten thousands place less than that of the number in the box?

    $$\boxed{5{,}625{,}609}$$

    F 7,725,817
    G 3,443,715
    H 1,531,512
    J 4,613,514

15. It cost Max $637.59 to have the roof of his house repaired. Rounded to the nearest ten dollars, how much did Max pay?

    A $600   C $640
    B $630   D $700

Addition

Reviewing Addition Concepts

Addition is the math term for putting things together.

• Questions often have words that signal addition.

Examples

Find five *plus* three.
Find the *total* of five and three.
What is the *sum* of five and three?

How much are five *and* three *in all*?
What is the result of five *added to* three?
How much are five and three *all together*?

• Numbers that are added together are **addends**.

• The result of an addition is called the **sum** or **total**.

• Addition can be written two ways:

vertically, in a **column**, from top to bottom

horizontally, in a **row**, from left to right ↔

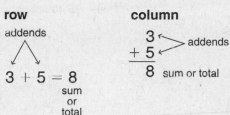

• Changing the order of the addends does not change the sum or total.
Each addition fact has a related addition fact in which the addends are switched.
  6 + 4 = 10   4 + 6 = 10

• Addition and subtraction are opposites.
There is a related subtraction fact for every addition fact.
  4 + 5 = 9 so 9 − 5 = 4   *and*   5 + 4 = 9 so 9 − 4 = 5

• If you add zero to a number, the value does not change.
  8 + 0 = 8

• Only like things can be added. To add tables and desks you would have to name them in the same way, for example, as pieces of furniture.

PRACTICE

Complete.

1. Write three related sentences for 12 + 19 = 31.

   _____

   _____

   _____

2. Circle the letter of the expression that has the same value as 265 + 57.

   A 265 − 57   **C** 57 − 265
   B 57 + 265   **D** None of these

3. Write *true* or *false*.
   2 flies + 3 ants = 5 ant-flies

   _____

4. 423 + 0 =   _____

Reviewing Basic Addition Facts

To solve problems using addition, you should be able to recall basic facts quickly and accurately.

PRACTICE

Find each sum. Correct errors and work on any facts you miss.

1. $2 + 3 =$ _____ $3 + 3 =$ _____ $7 + 7 =$ _____ $0 + 3 =$ _____

2. $8 + 8 =$ _____ $6 + 4 =$ _____ $2 + 2 =$ _____ $9 + 6 =$ _____

3. $1 + 1 =$ _____ $6 + 5 =$ _____ $6 + 3 =$ _____ $1 + 3 =$ _____

4. $5 + 2 =$ _____ $4 + 7 =$ _____ $0 + 0 =$ _____ $4 + 1 =$ _____

5.
$$\begin{array}{r} 4 \\ + 3 \\ \hline \end{array} \qquad \begin{array}{r} 7 \\ + 8 \\ \hline \end{array} \qquad \begin{array}{r} 4 \\ + 4 \\ \hline \end{array} \qquad \begin{array}{r} 8 \\ + 9 \\ \hline \end{array} \qquad \begin{array}{r} 9 \\ + 9 \\ \hline \end{array} \qquad \begin{array}{r} 4 \\ + 0 \\ \hline \end{array}$$

6.
$$\begin{array}{r} 7 \\ + 0 \\ \hline \end{array} \qquad \begin{array}{r} 7 \\ + 5 \\ \hline \end{array} \qquad \begin{array}{r} 3 \\ + 5 \\ \hline \end{array} \qquad \begin{array}{r} 2 \\ + 4 \\ \hline \end{array} \qquad \begin{array}{r} 1 \\ + 2 \\ \hline \end{array} \qquad \begin{array}{r} 3 \\ + 0 \\ \hline \end{array}$$

7.
$$\begin{array}{r} 5 \\ + 1 \\ \hline \end{array} \qquad \begin{array}{r} 6 \\ + 2 \\ \hline \end{array} \qquad \begin{array}{r} 1 \\ + 7 \\ \hline \end{array} \qquad \begin{array}{r} 8 \\ + 4 \\ \hline \end{array} \qquad \begin{array}{r} 6 \\ + 6 \\ \hline \end{array} \qquad \begin{array}{r} 3 \\ + 7 \\ \hline \end{array}$$

8.
$$\begin{array}{r} 8 \\ + 2 \\ \hline \end{array} \qquad \begin{array}{r} 3 \\ + 8 \\ \hline \end{array} \qquad \begin{array}{r} 0 \\ + 2 \\ \hline \end{array} \qquad \begin{array}{r} 1 \\ + 8 \\ \hline \end{array} \qquad \begin{array}{r} 5 \\ + 4 \\ \hline \end{array} \qquad \begin{array}{r} 0 \\ + 5 \\ \hline \end{array}$$

9.
$$\begin{array}{r} 9 \\ + 4 \\ \hline \end{array} \qquad \begin{array}{r} 5 \\ + 5 \\ \hline \end{array} \qquad \begin{array}{r} 8 \\ + 7 \\ \hline \end{array} \qquad \begin{array}{r} 6 \\ + 1 \\ \hline \end{array} \qquad \begin{array}{r} 8 \\ + 0 \\ \hline \end{array} \qquad \begin{array}{r} 0 \\ + 0 \\ \hline \end{array}$$

10.
$$\begin{array}{r} 8 \\ + 5 \\ \hline \end{array} \qquad \begin{array}{r} 9 \\ + 3 \\ \hline \end{array} \qquad \begin{array}{r} 7 \\ + 9 \\ \hline \end{array} \qquad \begin{array}{r} 0 \\ + 6 \\ \hline \end{array} \qquad \begin{array}{r} 5 \\ + 8 \\ \hline \end{array} \qquad \begin{array}{r} 9 \\ + 4 \\ \hline \end{array}$$

Adding Three or More Numbers

No matter how many digits there are, you can add only two digits at a time. You can start at the top of the column and work down. Add two digits, then add the next digit to that sum. However, you do not have to add in order. Remember that you can change the order of the addends and still get the same sum, so look for pairs that are easy for you to add.

Examples

$$\begin{array}{r} 1 \\ 2 \\ 5 \\ + \ 4 \\ \hline 12 \end{array}$$

Add the digits in order.
$1 + 2 = 3$
Then think: $3 + 5 = 8$
Finally, think: $8 + 4 = 12$

$$\begin{array}{r} 1 \\ 2 \\ 5 \\ + \ 4 \\ \hline 12 \end{array}$$

Look for easy facts.
$1 + 4 = 5$
Then think: $5 + 5 = 10$
Finally, think: $10 + 2 = 12$

You can check your work by adding in a different order.

PRACTICE

Find each sum. Then check your addition. If there are labels or decimal points, repeat them in your answer.

1.
11	13	2	4¢	16	224
20	5	3	12¢	12	52
+ 32	+ 1	+ 5	+ 2¢	+ 11	+ 11

2.
131	25 yd	42	7	4	8 in.
14	12 yd	53	3	2	2 in.
+ 22	+ 2 yd	+ 41	+ 1	+ 6	+ 5 in.

3.
3	4	10	15	$60	23
2	3	4	20	$30	31
6	6	+ 24	+ 23	+ $80	+ 41
+ 5	+ 2				

4.
31 in.	4	8	$ 6.10	12	430
23 in.	23	3	3.25	5	12
22 in.	+ 51	6	+ 4.33	71	+ 143
+ 43 in.		+ 2		+ 20	

Writing Numbers in Columns to Add

It is easier to find a sum when the addends are written one below the other. When the numbers are not written that way, rewrite them. Place ones below ones, tens below tens, hundreds below hundreds, and so on.

Example

Add 114 + 203 + 52.

- Write addends one below the other.
  Line up the digits in place-value **columns**.
- Add the digits in one column at a time.
  Start adding in the ones column at right and work to the left.

114 + 203 + 52 = 369

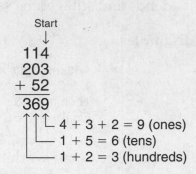

PRACTICE

Find each sum. Rewrite the addends in columns making sure to line up the digits. If there are dollar signs and decimal points, repeat them in the answer. Check your answers.

1. 21 + 73 = _____

2. 660 + 22 = _____

3. 40 + 125 = _____

4. $60.50 + $25.25 = _____

5. 1,344 + 634 = _____

6. 902 + 56 + 40 = _____

7. 130 + 51 = _____

8. 430 + 309 = _____

9. 602 + 215 = _____

10. 1,303 + 5,251 = _____

11. 5,210 + 250 = _____

12. 552 + 26 = _____

13. 82 + 104 + 12 = _____

14. 77 + 101 + 20 = _____

15. 74 + 125 = _____

16. 335 + 430 = _____

Regrouping in Addition

When the sum of the digits in a column is **10** or more, **regroup** 10 of those units for 1 unit of the next greater value.

10 ones = 1 ten	10 hundreds = 1 thousand
10 tens = 1 hundred	10 thousands = 1 ten thousand

When you regroup, you record the digit for the greater unit in the next column to the left. This procedure is often called **carrying**. The digit that you carry is added with the digits in that column.

Sometimes you will group only once. You may regroup 10 ones to a ten, or 10 tens to a hundred, or 10 hundreds to a thousand, and so on.

Examples

Regrouping ones

Add 625 + 57.

```
   1
  625
+  57
  682
```
5 + 7 = 12 (ones)
12 ones = 1 ten + 2 ones
Write 2 (ones) in the answer.
Write 1 (ten) at the top of the tens column.
1 + 2 + 5 = 8 (tens)
6 + nothing = 6 (hundreds)

The sum is 682.

Regrouping tens

Add 384 + 53.

```
   1
  384
+  53
  437
```
4 + 3 = 7 (ones)
8 + 5 = 13 (tens)
13 tens = 1 hundred + 3 tens
Write 3 (tens) in the answer.
Write 1 (hundred) in the hundreds column
1 + 3 = 4 (hundreds)

The sum is 437.

PRACTICE

Find each sum. If there are labels or dollar signs and decimal points in a problem, repeat them in the answer. Be sure to check your work.

1.
59	88	55	125	1,050
+ 7	+ 30	+ 15	+ 65	+ 75

2.
68 gal	10,602	99 cans	59 in.	90
+ 203 gal	+ 900	+ 8 cans	+ 213 in.	+ 30

3.
32 miles	5,009	134	649 in.	761
+ 193 miles	+ 919	+ 82	+ 270 in.	+ 57

4.
290	$15.50	150	657	319
+ 230	+ 25.00	+ 90	+ 75	+ 4

Regrouping in Addition (continued)

Sometimes you need to regroup more than once. It is important to record the number you carry and add it with the digits in that column.

Example   Regrouping tens and ones

Add 3,282 + 618.

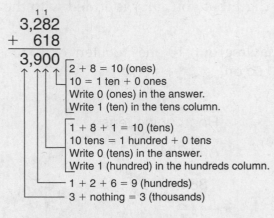

$$
\begin{array}{r}
{}^{1\,1} \\
3,282 \\
+\ \ 618 \\
\hline
3,900
\end{array}
$$

2 + 8 = 10 (ones)
10 = 1 ten + 0 ones
Write 0 (ones) in the answer.
Write 1 (ten) in the tens column.

1 + 8 + 1 = 10 (tens)
10 tens = 1 hundred + 0 tens
Write 0 (tens) in the answer.
Write 1 (hundred) in the hundreds column.

1 + 2 + 6 = 9 (hundreds)
3 + nothing = 3 (thousands)

3,282 + 618 = 3,900

PRACTICE

Find each sum. Rewrite each problem in column form making sure to line up digits in their place-value columns. For money problems, line up decimal points, and write decimal points and dollar signs in the answers. Be sure to check your work.

5. $17 + $18 = _____

6. 146 + 85 = _____

7. $1.23 + $0.67 = _____

8. 642 + 59 = _____

9. 700 + 500 = _____

10. $42 + $83 = _____

11. $2.25 + $0.15 = _____

12. 2,405 + 705 = _____

13. 55 + 475 = _____

14. $6.50 + $1.75 = _____

15. 163 + 459 = _____

16. 365 + 87 = _____

17. 2,670 + 2,430 = _____

18. 2,715 + 4,507 = _____

Using Estimation to Check Addition

You can check addition by using common sense or by adding the digits in each column in a different order. Another method to use is **front-end estimation**.

- Add only the digits in the far left column.
- Record the sum.
- Write a zero in each column to the right of the sum.

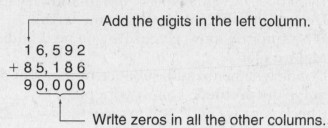

Add the digits in the left column.

```
  16,592
+ 85,186
  90,000
```

Write zeros in all the other columns. The estimate is 90,000.

When you use **front-end estimation**, the exact answer will always be **greater than** your estimate.

PRACTICE

Estimate each sum using the first digit of each number. *Remember:* With front-end estimation, your estimate should have at least as many places as the greatest number in the problem.

1.
```
    7,312          5,527         91 yards         $66.89
 +  6,903       +  6,301       + 73 yards       +$12.43
```

2.
```
      549         20,212          1,893            257
 +    315      +  13,500       +  4,615         +   13
```

Circle the letter of the *best* estimate for each problem.

3.
```
  115
+ 617
```
A 600
B exactly 700
C less than 700
D more than 700

6.
```
  1,052
+   359
```
F 1,000
G 2,000
H 4,000
J   900

4. 6,785 + 4,609 = _____

F 6,000
G 4,000
H more than 10,000
J less than 10,000

7.
```
  6,840
+ 1,193
```
A more than 7,000
B more than 70,000
C less than 7,000
D exactly 70,000

5. $3.97 + $5.12 = _____

A less than $3
B more than $8
C less than $5
D less than $8

8. $5.63 + $8.19 = _____

F less than $13
G more than $1.30
H more than $13
J less than $1.30

Working with Word Problems

Here are five steps to follow that will help you with word problems.
- **Identify the question**.
  What does the problem ask you to find? Try to put the question in your own words.
- **Determine what information you need**.
  What information is given? Do you need additional information?
- **Make a plan**.
  Decide whether to add, subtract, multiply, or divide. Look for clue words that can help you.
- **Solve the problem**. Follow your plan.
- **Check your work**.
  Did you answer the question?
  Does your answer make sense? Is it reasonable?
  Is your computation correct?

PRACTICE

Underline the question to be answered in each problem below.
Then circle the number of each problem that calls for addition.
You do not need to solve the problems, but be prepared to explain your choices.
Hint: Some words that signal addition can be found on page 15.

1. Quinton just bought a bed that is 7 feet long. His bedroom is 10 feet long. If he puts the bed against one wall, how much space will be left between the end of his bed and the other wall?

2. At rush hour, the Busy Bee Cafe has 4 waitresses, 1 dishwasher, 2 cooks, 2 busboys, and 1 manager. How many people in all work at the Busy Bee during rush hour?

3. People in Renee's neighborhood have started putting ceramic geese in their yards. Renee counted 12 geese on her block and 9 geese on the next block. How many geese is that in all?

4. It costs 50 cents to play a game of "Paratroopers Attack!" How many games can you play for $5?

5. The speed limit is 40 miles an hour. Alex is driving 25 miles an hour. How far under the speed limit is he driving?

6. Monte bought a cheesecake for $8.15 and a coffeecake for $6.98. Tax was $1.20. What was the total cost?

7. Two companies share a parking lot. One company has 14 employees. The other has 52 employees. Each employee gets 1 parking space. What is the least number of parking spaces the parking lot must have?

8. Tori won $25 playing bingo, but she spent $7.50 on bingo cards. How much money did she have after she subtracted the cost of the bingo cards?

Use the information below to solve Numbers 9–12. Check your answers using front-end estimation.

The dining room at the Busy Bee Cafe seats 250 people. There are seats for another 23 people at the counter. Today's specials are the hot beef sandwich for $4.45 and the meatloaf dinner for $5.50.

9. If every seat is filled, how many people can sit at the Busy Bee?

10. How much would it cost to buy two hot beef sandwiches? (Ignore the tax.)

11. Tax on the meatloaf dinner is $0.45. What is the total cost of a meatloaf dinner?

12. The salad bar costs $2.50 extra. How much would it cost to buy the meatloaf dinner with the salad bar? (Ignore the tax.)

Sometimes you have to find missing information before you can solve a problem. Tell what information is needed to solve each problem.

13. Mr. Nguyen bought a shirt and spent $15.95 on gas. How much did he spend in all?

You also need to know _____

_____

14. Kali's cat gained 2 pounds this year. How much does it weigh now?

You also need to know _____

_____

15. When Wendy bought her car, she paid an extra $850 for air conditioning. What was the total cost of the car?

You also need to know _____

_____

16. Frederick's insurance payment went up $35. How much does he pay now?

You also need to know _____

_____

Addition Skills Checkup

Circle the letter for the correct answer to each problem.

1.

      2,378
    + 1,321

   A 3,679
   B 3,099
   C 3,659
   D 3,699
   E None of these

2.

      1,876
    +   8

   F 1,874
   G 1,884
   H 1,076
   J 1,878
   K None of these

3. $516 + 29 =$

   A 545
   B 535
   C 806
   D 525
   E None of these

4. $16 + 402 + 31 =$

   F 548
   G 718
   H 448
   J 449
   K None of these

5.

      2,183
    + 4,064

   A 2,247
   B 7,247
   C 6,147
   D 7,147
   E None of these

Use this information to do Numbers 6–8.

Marshall is 62 miles from Lincoln.
Lincoln is 43 miles from Rush.
Rush is 39 miles from Calloway.

6. You must drive from Lincoln to Rush and then back again. How far will you drive?

   F 62 miles
   G 43 miles
   H 45 miles
   J 86 miles

7. Jordan is driving from Marshall to Lincoln to see his parents, then on to Rush to visit a friend. How long will his trip be?

   A 62 miles
   B 43 miles
   C 105 miles
   D 15 miles

8. This month, Sarah took two trips. One was to Marshall and back. The other was to Rush and back. If Sarah lives in Lincoln, how many miles did these two trips put on her car?

   F 105 miles
   G 210 miles
   H 148 miles
   J 167 miles

9.

462
+ 163

A 525
B 625
C 615
D 626
E None of these

10.

3,462
+ 1,875

F 5,237
G 5,347
H 5,337
J 4,237
K None of these

11.

$2.90
+ 1.85

A $4.75
B $3.75
C $4.70
D $4.85
E None of these

12.

5 + 5 + 9 =

F 9
G 19
H 15
J 18
K None of these

13.

80
+ 25

A 95
B 100
C 115
D 125
E None of these

14.

$0.20 + $1.45 + $5 =

F $5.65
G $8.45
H $6.65
J $6.47
K None of these

15. Which of these has the same value as 10 + 9?

A 1 + 0 + 9
B 6 + 4 + 9
C 10 + 3 + 3
D 9 + 1 + 8

16. Which of these shows regrouping for 12 tens?

F 1 ten + 2 ones
G 1 hundred + 2 ones
H 1 hundred + 2 tens
J 1 thousand + 2 hundreds

17. Which of the following amounts is different from the others?

A 25 cents + 75 cents
B ten dimes
C 50 cents + 50 cents
D ten nickels and one quarter

18. Which of these *does not* have the same value as 52 + 29?

F 29 + 52
G 52 + 29 + 1
H 52 + 29 + 0
J   52
    + 29

19. Which of the following phrases represents 12 + 7?

A twelve groups of seven
B one-seventh of twelve
C twelve minus seven
D the total of twelve and seven

Subtraction

Reviewing Subtraction Concepts

Subtraction is the term for taking something away or for comparing two amounts to find the difference between them.

- Questions often have words that signal subtraction.

Examples
What is 50 *minus* 12?
What is the *difference* between 50 and 12?
Joe has $50. If he spends $12, *how much will be left*?
Joe has $12. *How much more* does he need to buy a sweater that costs $50?
Sam has $12. Joe has $50. *How much less* money does Sam have?
Joe's owes $12. He gives the clerk a $50 bill. *How much change* should he get?

- The answer in a subtraction problem is called the **difference**.

- Subtraction can be written two ways:

  horizontally, in a **row** from left to right $\longleftrightarrow$

  vertically, in a **column** from top to bottom $\updownarrow$

  row
  $$15 - 10 = \underset{\uparrow \atop \text{difference}}{5}$$

  column
  $$\begin{array}{r} 15 \\ -\ 10 \\ \hline 5 \end{array} \leftarrow \text{difference}$$

- If you change the order of the numbers in a subtraction problem, the answer will *not* be the same.
  $$8 - 5 \neq 5 - 8 \quad \text{Note: } \neq \text{ means } not \text{ equal.}$$

- If you subtract 0 from a number, the value does not change. $7 - 0 = 7$

- If you subtract a number from itself, the difference is 0. $7 - 7 = 0$

- For every subtraction fact, there is a related subtraction fact that uses the same numbers.

  ⊗⊗⊗⊗⊗○○○○   ⊗⊗⊗⊗○○○○○
  $$9 - 5 = 4 \qquad\qquad 9 - 4 = 5$$

- Subtraction is the opposite of addition. There are two related addition facts for each subtraction fact.
  $$9 - 5 = 4 \quad \text{so} \quad 5 + 4 = 9 \quad and \quad 4 + 5 = 9$$

- Only *like* things can be subtracted. You can subtract apples from apples and oranges from oranges, but you cannot subtract apples from oranges.

PRACTICE

Write T for *true* or F for *false*.

1. $567 - 98 = 98 - 567$ _____

2. $367 - 367 = 0$ _____

3. $8,932 - 0 = 8,932$ _____

4. The same number can go in both boxes: _____
   If $8 - \square = 5$, then $5 + \square = 8$.

Reviewing Basic Subtraction Facts

To be able to solve subtraction problems quickly and efficiently, you need to know basic subtraction facts. You can use a related addition fact you know to help you with subtraction.

Example

$$10 - 8 = \square$$

Think: $8 + \square = 10$
$8 + 2 = 10$, so $\square = 2$.

$$\begin{array}{r} 10 \\ -\ 8 \\ \hline \square \end{array}$$

PRACTICE

Find each difference.

1. $8 - 6 =$ _____ $7 - 3 =$ _____ $10 - 5 =$ _____

2. $6 - 4 =$ _____ $10 - 2 =$ _____ $9 - 6 =$ _____

3. $10 - 1 =$ _____ $6 - 5 =$ _____ $6 - 3 =$ _____

4. $5 - 2 =$ _____ $7 - 4 =$ _____ $3 - 2 =$ _____

5.
$$\begin{array}{r} 4 \\ -3 \\ \hline \end{array} \quad \begin{array}{r} 8 \\ -7 \\ \hline \end{array} \quad \begin{array}{r} 4 \\ -4 \\ \hline \end{array} \quad \begin{array}{r} 9 \\ -8 \\ \hline \end{array} \quad \begin{array}{r} 9 \\ -3 \\ \hline \end{array} \quad \begin{array}{r} 4 \\ -0 \\ \hline \end{array} \quad \begin{array}{r} 5 \\ -5 \\ \hline \end{array}$$

6.
$$\begin{array}{r} 10 \\ -4 \\ \hline \end{array} \quad \begin{array}{r} 7 \\ -5 \\ \hline \end{array} \quad \begin{array}{r} 5 \\ -3 \\ \hline \end{array} \quad \begin{array}{r} 4 \\ -2 \\ \hline \end{array} \quad \begin{array}{r} 2 \\ -1 \\ \hline \end{array} \quad \begin{array}{r} 3 \\ -0 \\ \hline \end{array} \quad \begin{array}{r} 6 \\ -1 \\ \hline \end{array}$$

7.
$$\begin{array}{r} 5 \\ -1 \\ \hline \end{array} \quad \begin{array}{r} 6 \\ -2 \\ \hline \end{array} \quad \begin{array}{r} 7 \\ -1 \\ \hline \end{array} \quad \begin{array}{r} 8 \\ -4 \\ \hline \end{array} \quad \begin{array}{r} 7 \\ -6 \\ \hline \end{array} \quad \begin{array}{r} 10 \\ -3 \\ \hline \end{array} \quad \begin{array}{r} 9 \\ -3 \\ \hline \end{array}$$

8.
$$\begin{array}{r} 8 \\ -2 \\ \hline \end{array} \quad \begin{array}{r} 8 \\ -3 \\ \hline \end{array} \quad \begin{array}{r} 10 \\ -2 \\ \hline \end{array} \quad \begin{array}{r} 8 \\ -1 \\ \hline \end{array} \quad \begin{array}{r} 5 \\ -4 \\ \hline \end{array} \quad \begin{array}{r} 5 \\ -0 \\ \hline \end{array} \quad \begin{array}{r} 10 \\ -6 \\ \hline \end{array}$$

9.
$$\begin{array}{r} 9 \\ -4 \\ \hline \end{array} \quad \begin{array}{r} 10 \\ -7 \\ \hline \end{array} \quad \begin{array}{r} 8 \\ -0 \\ \hline \end{array} \quad \begin{array}{r} 8 \\ -5 \\ \hline \end{array} \quad \begin{array}{r} 9 \\ -7 \\ \hline \end{array} \quad \begin{array}{r} 9 \\ -5 \\ \hline \end{array} \quad \begin{array}{r} 0 \\ -0 \\ \hline \end{array}$$

Writing Numbers in Columns to Subtract

It is easier to find a difference when the numbers are written one below the other. When problems are not written that way, rewrite them. Place ones below ones, tens below tens, and so on.

Example   Subtract 352 − 322.

- Write the number you are subtracting *from* on top.
- Write the amount you are subtracting on the bottom. Line up digits in columns.
- Start subtracting in the ones column at right and work to the left.
- Always subtract the number on the bottom from the number on the top.

$$352 - 322 = 30$$

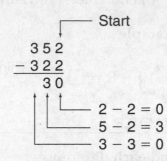

You do not write a zero at the left of a whole number.

You can use addition to check your answers. When you add the number you subtracted and the difference, the sum should match the starting number.

Problem	Check
352	322
− 322	+ 30
30	352

OK

PRACTICE

Rewrite each subtraction problem in column form. Then find each difference. **Be sure to check your work. If numbers in a problem have labels or decimal points, repeat them in your answer. (*Note*: Line up decimal points in money problems.)**

1. 870 − 620 = _____

2. 462 − 31 = _____

3. 7,910 − 500 = _____

4. 231 miles − 220 miles = _____

5. 558 − 42 = _____

6. 1,375 − 32 = _____

7. 5,400 − 3,100 = _____

8. 1,050 − 1,020 = _____

9. $3.45 − $1.32 = _____

10. 1,947 − 823 = _____

11. $25 − $15 = _____

12. 86 in. − 32 in. = _____

13. $17.89 − $15.62 = _____

14. 487 − 25 = _____

Regrouping in Subtraction

When you subtract, you always subtract the bottom number from the top number. If the digit you are subtracting is greater than the digit you are subtracting from, you can get more of the units you need by regrouping. This procedure is often called **borrowing**.

1 ten = 10 ones   1 thousand = 10 hundreds
1 hundred = 10 tens   1 ten thousand = 10 thousands

You always regroup, or borrow, from the column just left of the one you are working with. It is important to record your steps to help you keep track of the numbers you are working with. Be sure to subtract from the numbers you record after you regroup.

Examples   Regrouping tens and ones

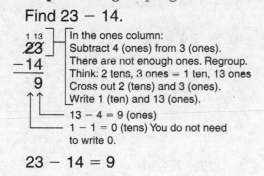

Find 23 − 14.

1 13
2̶3̶
−14
  9

In the ones column:
Subtract 4 (ones) from 3 (ones).
There are not enough ones. Regroup.
Think: 2 tens, 3 ones = 1 ten, 13 ones
Cross out 2 (tens) and 3 (ones).
Write 1 (ten) and 13 (ones).
  13 − 4 = 9 (ones)
  1 − 1 = 0 (tens) You do not need to write 0.

23 − 14 = 9

Find 4,501 − 160.

4 10
4,5̶0̶1
− 160
4,341

In the tens column:
Subtract 6 (tens) from 0 (tens).
There are 0 tens. Regroup.
Think: 5 hundreds, 0 tens = 4 hundreds, 10 tens
Cross out 5 (hundreds) and 0 (tens).
Write 4 (hundreds) and 10 (tens).
  1 − 0 = 1 (ones)
  10 − 6 = 4 (tens)
  4 − 1 = 3 (hundreds)
  4 − 0 = 4 (thousands)

4,501 − 160 = 4,341

PRACTICE

Find each difference. If there are labels or dollar signs and decimal points, remember to repeat them in the answer. Be sure to check your work.

1. 82
    − 8

2. 142
    − 15

3. 618
    − 26

4. $1.07
    −$0.35

5. 917
    − 891

6. 1,540 meters
    −   7 meters

7. 1,940 feet
    − 903 feet

8. $12.50
    −$ 1.25

9. $15.50
    −$14.25

10. 890
     − 27

11. 3,652   591 −

12. 712 − 29 =

13. 991 − 85 =

14. 384 − 75 =

15. 978 − 59 =

16. $1.61 − $0.32 =

Regrouping in Subtraction (continued)

Sometimes you need to regroup more than once. If you have already crossed out a number, use the new number you have written above it. Make sure you record each step, and be sure to subtract from the new numbers you have written.

Examples   Find 1,831 − 249.

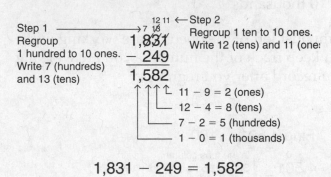

Step 1
Regroup
1 hundred to 10 ones.
Write 7 (hundreds)
and 13 (tens)

12 11 ← Step 2
7 13
1,831
− 249
1,582

Step 2
Regroup 1 ten to 10 ones.
Write 12 (tens) and 11 (ones).

11 − 9 = 2 (ones)
12 − 4 = 8 (tens)
7 − 2 = 5 (hundreds)
1 − 0 = 1 (thousands)

1,831 − 249 = 1,582

Find 407 − 39.

Step 1
Regroup 1 hundred to 10 tens.
Write 3 (hundreds) and 10 (tens).

3 10
9 17
407
− 39
368

Step 2
Regroup 1 ten to 10 ones.
Write 9 (tens) and 17 (ones).

17 − 9 = 8 (ones)
9 − 3 = 6 (tens)
3 − 0 = 3 (hundreds)

407 − 39 = 368

PRACTICE

Find each difference.

17. 306
     − 9

18. 800
     − 8

19. 205
     − 76

20. 400
     − 72

21. 264
     − 187

22. 1,342
     − 283

23. 903
     − 537

24. 3,100
     − 56

25. 6,233
     − 1,097

26. 856
     − 478

27. 3,304
     − 165

28. 760
     − 382

29. 1,547
     − 488

30. 645
     − 97

31. 5,403
     − 327

Using Estimation to Check Subtraction

When you estimate, you find out *about* how much — you do not find an exact answer. Here are two different ways to estimate a difference.

Front-End Estimation

Subtract.
```
  6,9 4 2
– 1,2 4 6
  5,0 0 0
```
Write zeros.

- One method uses **front-end estimation**. Subtract the digits in the column at the left. Then write zeros in all the other columns.

- Another method uses **rounding**. Round each number to its greatest place. Then subtract using the rounded numbers.

Rounding

$$6,942 \rightarrow 7,000$$
$$1,246 \rightarrow -1,000$$
$$6,000$$

PRACTICE

Use front-end estimation to find each difference.

1. $25.91
    – $12.03

2. $512.14
  – $211.91

3. 25,921 – 3,412 =

4. $67.44 – $39 =

5. 71,892 – 25,912 =

6. 877 – 3 =

Round each number to its greatest place. Then find the difference of the rounded numbers.

7.   4,192
    – 1,527

8.   3,192
    – 1,890

9.   92,705
    – 32,905

10. $35.98
   – $11.05

11.   8,221
   – 997

12.   497 feet
  – 97 feet

Round each amount to the nearest dollar. Then find the difference of the rounded amounts.

13. $19.21 $13.42

14. $75.89 $38.79

15. $61.85 $39.99

16. $6.99 $2.97

Round each amount to the nearest ten dollars. Then find the difference of the rounded amounts.

17. $37.50 $8.75

18. $301.62 $45.50

Working with Word Problems

You can use these five steps to solve word problems.

- Identify the question.
- Determine what information you need.
- Make a plan.
- Solve the problem. Follow your plan.
- Check your work.

PRACTICE

Circle the letter of the phrases that tell what you need to find to answer the question. Then find the answer. *Remember*: **For subtraction, you take away something or find a difference. For addition, you combine amounts.**

1. Zeke spent $12.89 on gas. He paid with a $20 bill. About how much change should he get back?

   A an exact sum
   B an exact difference
   C an estimated difference
   D an estimated sum

   _____

2. Diego bought 2 crates of potato chips. Each crate contains 52 bags of chips. Approximately how many bags of chips did he buy?

   F an exact sum
   G an exact difference
   H an estimated difference
   J an estimated sum

   _____

3. Martin bought 50 pounds of potatoes. He has 15 pounds of potatoes left. How many pounds have been used?

   A an exact sum
   B an exact difference
   C an estimated difference
   D an estimated sum

   _____

4. There are just over 210 days in the school year. This is the 175th day of school. About how many days of school are left?

   F an exact sum
   G an exact difference
   H an estimated difference
   J an estimated sum

   _____

5. Ann's hair is 12 inches long. If it grows 2 inches, how long will it be?

   A an exact sum
   B an exact difference
   C an estimated difference
   D an estimated sum

   _____

6. Last month there was $1,542 in Johanna's bank account. This month the account balance is $1,837. How much money did Johanna save this month?

   F an exact sum
   G an exact difference
   H an estimated difference
   J an estimated sum

   _____

Use the information below to solve Numbers 7–10. Then use estimation to check whether your answer is reasonable. *Remember*: You can add or subtract only like things.

> Edwardo's company has 892 packages to deliver. Of those, 381 will go to addresses in town. The rest are going to areas nearby. A driver working in town can deliver 35 packages a day. A driver working in the nearby areas can deliver about 15 packages a day.

7. How many packages will be delivered to nearby areas?

9. Edwardo's workers deliver 559 packages on the first day. How many packages are left to be delivered?

8. How many more packages can be delivered in town in a day than can be delivered to the nearby areas?

10. About how many packages can be delivered both in town and to the nearby areas in one day?

These word problems do not give enough information. Tell what information is needed to solve each problem.

11. Eddie has only $5.10 left in his wallet. How much has he spent?

You also need to know _____

_____

12. Arlene has saved $253 to pay for a new dining room set. How much more does she need to save?

You also need to know _____

_____

13. Sandy bought 400 pounds of cement to build a patio. He will use whatever is left over to build a small fish pond. How much cement will he have left for the pond?

You also need to know _____

_____

14. Sylvia was caught in a traffic jam today. It took her 96 minutes to drive to work. How much longer than her usual drive was today's drive?

You also need to know _____

_____

Subtraction Skills Checkup

Circle the letter of the correct answer to each problem.

1.
$$395 - 142$$
A 243
B 252
C 242
D 253
E None of these

2.
$$2,342 - 331$$
F 2,011
G 2,042
H 2,111
J 2,311
K None of these

3.
$$507 - 63$$
A 444
B 544
C 443
D 545
E None of these

4.
$$5,419 - 170$$
F 5,369
G 5,349
H 5,249
J 5,449
K None of these

5.
$$2,450 - 14 =$$
A 2,310
B 1,050
C 2,446
D 2,436
E None of these

6.
$$96 - 42 =$$
F 54
G 45
H 52
J 53
K None of these

7. Kyle is driving 2,850 miles from New York to Los Angeles. He has already traveled 1,687 miles. How much farther does he need to drive?

A 1,237 miles
B 1,273 miles
C 1,433 miles
D 1,163 miles

Use the information below to answer Numbers 8–10.

Trina took $50 out of the bank. She spent $12.50 of that money on gasoline.

8. What would you do to find how much money Trina had left?

F add
G divide
H multiply
J subtract

9. Trina then gave $3.50 to her daughter for lunch. How much has Trina spent altogether?

A $53.50
B $15.50
C $16
D $66

10. Before she withdrew the money, Tina had $1,479 in her account. How much money was in the account after she withdrew $50?

F $1,528
G $1,474
H $ 979
J $1,429

11.
88
$-$ 62

A 26
B 16
C 27
D 25
E None of these

12.
$12
$-$ $8

F $ 0.40
G $ 4
H $40
J $ 4.50
K None of these

13.
5,376
$-$ 1,354

A   422
B 4,022
C 4,021
D 4,032
E None of these

14.
6,850
$-$ 5,350

F 1,500
G   150
H 1,050
J 1,550
K None of these

15.
1,090
$-$ 805

A 290
B 210
C 295
D 285
E None of these

16.
$607 - 90 =$

F 517
G 617
H 697
J 597
K None of these

17. Which of the following is false?

A $1,679 - 1,679 = 0$
B If $97 - 18 = 79$,
then $79 + 18 = 97$.
C $27 - 0 = 0$
D 5 tens = 4 tens + 10 ones

18. What number goes in the box to make the second number sentence true?

$345 + 52 = 397$

$397 - \square = 345$

F   52
G 397
H 342
J It is impossible to tell.

19. Which of these, if any, has the same value as $37 - 9$?

A $9 - 37$
B $37 - 9 - 0$
C $37 - 9 - 1$
D None of these

20. Which of the following phrases represents $89 - 25$?

F twenty-five less than eighty-nine
G eighty-nine divided by twenty-five
H eighty-nine subtracted from twenty-five
J eighty-nine more than twenty-five

Multiplication

Reviewing Basic Multiplication Concepts

You can think of **multiplication** as a shortcut for adding the same number several times. For example, $9 + 9 + 9 + 9 + 9$ is 5 groups of 9 *or* 5×9.

- Questions often have words that signal multiplication.

Examples

The second jump was *twice* as long as the first.   The seven pencils cost 49 cents *apiece*.
Each number was *multiplied* by five.   Boyce swam the length of the pool 5 *times*.
Each one weighed 10 pounds.

- Numbers that are multiplied are called **factors**.

- The result of multiplication is called a **product**.

- Multiplication can be written two ways:

  horizontally, in a row $\longleftrightarrow$

  vertically, in a column

$$
\begin{array}{cc}
\text{row} & \text{column} \\
\underset{\text{factors}}{7 \times 9} = \underset{\text{product}}{63} & \begin{array}{r} 9 \\ \times\ 7 \\ \hline 63 \end{array} \ \text{factors} \\
& \ \text{product}
\end{array}
$$

- If you change the order of the factors when you multiply, the product will not change.
  $5 \times 7 = 35$ and $7 \times 5 = 35$

- If there are more than two factors, you can group the factors to multiply them in a different order and the product will be the same.
  $4 \times 5 \times 2 = 4 \times (5 \times 2)$ and $4 \times 5 \times 2 = (4 \times 5) \times 2$
  $ = 4 \times 10 = 40$ $ = 20 \times 2 = 40$

- If you multiply any amount by zero, the product will be zero.
  $0 \times 13 = 0$ and $13 \times 0 = 0$

- If you multiply any amount by 1, its value will not change.
  $1 \times 425 = 425$ and $425 \times 1 = 425$

PRACTICE

Write T for *true* or F for *false*.

_____ 1. $37 + 37 + 37 = 3 \times 37$

_____ 2. $236 \times 0 = 236$

_____ 3. $2 \times 9 = 9 \times 2$

_____ 4. $8 \times (2 \times 4) = 8 \times 8$

_____ 5. $93 \times 1 = 93$

_____ 6. $0 \times 3 \times 5 = 0$

_____ 7. In the sentence $5 \times 4 = 20$, the factors are 5 and 4.

_____ 8. The product of 8×4 is 32.

_____ 9. $(7 \times 4) \times 5 = 7 \times (4 \times 5)$

_____ 10. 23×19 is the same as $\begin{array}{r} 23 \\ \times\ 19 \\ \hline \end{array}$

Reviewing Basic Multiplication Facts

Solving problems that involve multiplication is much easier when you know the basic multiplication facts. Work on any facts that you cannot recall quickly and accurately.

PRACTICE

Find each product.

1. $2 \times 6 =$ _____ $4 \times 4 =$ _____ $3 \times 9 =$ _____ $7 \times 8 =$ _____

2. $2 \times 3 =$ _____ $8 \times 4 =$ _____ $6 \times 6 =$ _____ $9 \times 6 =$ _____

3. $6 \times 5 =$ _____ $5 \times 3 =$ _____ $7 \times 6 =$ _____ $4 \times 9 =$ _____

4. $4 \times 2 =$ _____ $7 \times 4 =$ _____ $8 \times 9 =$ _____ $6 \times 8 =$ _____

5.
$$\begin{array}{r} 4 \\ \times\ 3 \\ \hline \end{array} \qquad \begin{array}{r} 2 \\ \times\ 2 \\ \hline \end{array} \qquad \begin{array}{r} 7 \\ \times\ 3 \\ \hline \end{array} \qquad \begin{array}{r} 3 \\ \times\ 9 \\ \hline \end{array}$$

6.
$$\begin{array}{r} 7 \\ \times\ 7 \\ \hline \end{array} \qquad \begin{array}{r} 8 \\ \times\ 3 \\ \hline \end{array} \qquad \begin{array}{r} 3 \\ \times\ 3 \\ \hline \end{array} \qquad \begin{array}{r} 4 \\ \times\ 5 \\ \hline \end{array}$$

7.
$$\begin{array}{r} 5 \\ \times\ 9 \\ \hline \end{array} \qquad \begin{array}{r} 7 \\ \times\ 5 \\ \hline \end{array} \qquad \begin{array}{r} 2 \\ \times\ 7 \\ \hline \end{array} \qquad \begin{array}{r} 4 \\ \times\ 6 \\ \hline \end{array}$$

8.
$$\begin{array}{r} 8 \\ \times\ 2 \\ \hline \end{array} \qquad \begin{array}{r} 2 \\ \times\ 9 \\ \hline \end{array} \qquad \begin{array}{r} 8 \\ \times\ 5 \\ \hline \end{array} \qquad \begin{array}{r} 8 \\ \times\ 8 \\ \hline \end{array}$$

9.
$$\begin{array}{r} 9 \\ \times\ 4 \\ \hline \end{array} \qquad \begin{array}{r} 7 \\ \times\ 8 \\ \hline \end{array} \qquad \begin{array}{r} 5 \\ \times\ 5 \\ \hline \end{array} \qquad \begin{array}{r} 6 \\ \times\ 8 \\ \hline \end{array}$$

10.
$$\begin{array}{r} 7 \\ \times\ 9 \\ \hline \end{array} \qquad \begin{array}{r} 3 \\ \times\ 6 \\ \hline \end{array} \qquad \begin{array}{r} 9 \\ \times\ 9 \\ \hline \end{array} \qquad \begin{array}{r} 6 \\ \times\ 9 \\ \hline \end{array}$$

Multiplying by a One-Digit Factor

When factors are written one below the other, the digits should be in their place-value columns.

- Multiply the number on top by the number on the bottom.
- Multiply each digit in the top number. Start with the digit at the right and working to the left.

Example

```
  3 4
×   2  ←——— Multiply by this digit.
  6 8
```

2 × 4 (ones) = 8 (ones)
2 × 3 (tens) = 6 (tens)

When multiplying money, be sure to place the dollar sign and decimal point in the answer. The decimal point should have 2 digits after it.

Example

```
$ 3.30
×    2
$ 6.60
```

decimal point

PRACTICE

Find each product. If one of the factors has a label, repeat the label in your answer.
Hint: Write every digit in a product, even if it is a zero.

1.
```
    24        232        $1.22         31      41 inches
  × 2        × 3        × 4         × 5         × 6
```

2.
```
   204      81 feet     $1.00         74         920
  × 2       × 5        × 9         × 2         × 3
```

Rewrite each problem in column form. Then find the product. Check over work to make sure it is correct.

3. 214 × 2 = _____

6. 810 × 5 = _____

9. $9.44 × 2 = _____

4. 3 × 43 = _____

7. 33 × 3 = _____

10. 7,003 × 3 = _____

5. 5 × 70 = _____

8. $4.13 × 2 = _____

11. $8 × 8 = _____

Regrouping When You Multiply

If the product of two digits is 10 or greater, regroup. The procedure in multiplication is similar to what is done in addition. Study the examples.

Examples   Find 4×49.

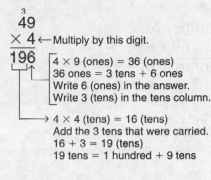

$$\overset{3}{4}9$$
$$\underline{\times\ 4} \leftarrow \text{Multiply by this digit.}$$
$$196$$

> 4×9 (ones) = 36 (ones)
> 36 ones = 3 tens + 6 ones
> Write 6 (ones) in the answer.
> Write 3 (tens) in the tens column.

> 4×4 (tens) = 16 (tens)
> Add the 3 tens that were carried.
> 16 + 3 = 19 (tens)
> 19 tens = 1 hundred + 9 tens

$$4 \times 49 = 156$$

Find 5×341.

$$\overset{2}{3}41$$
$$\underline{\times\quad 5} \leftarrow \text{Multiply by this digit.}$$
$$1{,}705$$

> 5×1 (one) = 5 (ones)
> Write 5 (ones) in the answer.

> 5×4 (tens) = 20 (tens)
> 20 tens = 2 hundreds + 0 tens
> Write 0 in the answer.
> Write 2 hundreds in the hundreds
>   column.

> 5×3 (hundreds) = 15 (hundreds)
> Add the 2 hundreds.
> 15 + 2 = 17 (hundreds)
> 17 hundreds = 1 thousand + 7 hundreds

$$5 \times 341 = 1{,}705$$

Note: Multiply first, then add the number that was carried from regrouping.

PRACTICE

Find each product.

1. $\begin{array}{r} 32 \\ \times\ 5 \\ \hline \end{array}$

2. $\begin{array}{r} 65 \\ \times\ 4 \\ \hline \end{array}$

3. $\begin{array}{r} 205 \\ \times\ 6 \\ \hline \end{array}$

4. $\begin{array}{r} 39 \\ \times\ 5 \\ \hline \end{array}$

5. $\begin{array}{r} 32 \\ \times\ 7 \\ \hline \end{array}$

6. $\begin{array}{r} 115 \\ \times\ 5 \\ \hline \end{array}$

7. $\begin{array}{r} 44 \\ \times\ 5 \\ \hline \end{array}$

8. $\begin{array}{r} 252 \\ \times\ 4 \\ \hline \end{array}$

9. $\begin{array}{r} 731 \\ \times\ 5 \\ \hline \end{array}$

10. $\begin{array}{r} 19 \\ \times\ 3 \\ \hline \end{array}$

11. $\begin{array}{r} 24 \\ \times\ 7 \\ \hline \end{array}$

12. $\begin{array}{r} 314 \\ \times\ 3 \\ \hline \end{array}$

13. $4 \times 308 =$ _____

14. $5 \times 28 =$ _____

15. $6 \times 95 =$ _____

16. $709 \times 7 =$ _____

17. $5 \times 25 =$ _____

18. $3 \times 243 =$ _____

Understanding Multiples

The numbers that are multiplied together are **factors**. The **product** is a **multiple** of each of the factors that were multiplied.

Examples

$3 \times 4 = 12$
12 is a multiple of 3.
12 is a multiple of 4.
3 and 4 are factors of 12.

$2 \times 3 \times 4 = 24$
24 is a multiple of 2.
24 is a multiple of 3.
24 is a multiple of 4.
2, 3, and 4 are factors of 24.

The first six multiples of 5 are 5, 10, 15, 20, 25, and 30.
The first six multiples of 10 are 10, 20, 30, 40, 50, and 60.

PRACTICE

List the next five multiples.

1. 9, 18, 27, _____, _____, _____, _____, _____

2. 25, 50, 75, _____, _____, _____, _____, _____

3. 20, 40, 60, _____, _____, _____, _____, _____

4. 11, 22, 33, _____, _____, _____, _____, _____

5. 7, 14, 21, _____, _____, _____, _____, _____

Circle the letter of the correct answer.

6. This number is a multiple of 6.

    A 15   C 28
    B 42   D 50

7. This number is a multiple of 8.

    F 24   H 36
    G 54   J 81

8. This number is a multiple of 12.

    A 18   C 24
    B 42   D 52

9. This number is a multiple of 100.

    F 350   H 520
    G 675   J 1,000

Write T for *true* or F for *false*.

_____ 10. 72 is a multiple of 8.

_____ 11. 56 is a multiple of 9.

_____ 12. 36 is a multiple of 4.

_____ 13. 6 and 8 are factors of 48.

_____ 14. 5 and 7 are factors of 12.

_____ 15. 9 and 8 are factors of 72.

Multiplying by 10s and 100s

Multiplying by 10s

To multiply a number by 10 or a multiple of 10 such as 20, 30, 40,...90, just multiply by the digit in the tens place and write one 0 after the product.

Example   Find 30 × 20.
Think 3 × 20 = 60, and then write 0 after the product to get 600.

Study the patterns in these examples.

1 × 6 = 6	2 × 6 = 12	1 × 15 = 15	2 × 15 = 30
10 × 6 = 60	20 × 6 = 120	10 × 15 = 150	20 × 15 = 300

Multiplying by 100s

To multiply a number by 100 or a multiple of 100 such as 200, 300, 400,...900, just multiply by the digit in the hundreds place and write two 0s after the product.

Example   Find 400 × 25.
Think 4 × 25 is 100, and then write two 0s after the product to get 10,000.

Study the patterns in these examples.

1 × 7 = 7	2 × 7 = 14	1 × 12 = 12	2 × 12 = 24
100 × 7 = 700	200 × 7 = 1,400	100 × 12 = 1,200	200 × 12 = 2,400

PRACTICE

Find each product. Remember, changing the order of the factors will not change the product.

1. 10 × 8 = _____

2. 100 × 4 = _____

3. 8 × 60 = _____

4. 47 × 10 = _____

5. 15 × 100 = _____

6. 4 × 700 = _____

7. 20 × 9 = _____

8. 8 × 700 = _____

9. 5 × 200 = _____

10. 2 × 90 = _____

11. 7 × 800 = _____

12. 500 × 2 = _____

13. $\begin{array}{r} 10 \\ \times\ 27 \\ \hline \end{array}$

14. $\begin{array}{r} 30 \\ \times\ 90 \\ \hline \end{array}$

15. $\begin{array}{r} 100 \\ \times\ 56 \\ \hline \end{array}$

16. $\begin{array}{r} 10 \\ \times\ 30 \\ \hline \end{array}$

17. $\begin{array}{r} 234 \\ \times\ 20 \\ \hline \end{array}$

18. $\begin{array}{r} 234 \\ \times\ 200 \\ \hline \end{array}$

19. $\begin{array}{r} 200 \\ \times\ 30 \\ \hline \end{array}$

20. $\begin{array}{r} 15 \\ \times\ 80 \\ \hline \end{array}$

21. $\begin{array}{r} 100 \\ \times\ 123 \\ \hline \end{array}$

22. $\begin{array}{r} 50 \\ \times\ 60 \\ \hline \end{array}$

23. $\begin{array}{r} 111 \\ \times\ 90 \\ \hline \end{array}$

24. $\begin{array}{r} 111 \\ \times\ 900 \\ \hline \end{array}$

Multiplying by a Two-Digit Factor

When you multiply by a two-digit number, you actually do two separate multiplication problems plus an addition problem.

- First, multiply by the digit in the ones place.
- Next, multiply by the digits in the tens place.
- Then, add the two products together.

Example Multiply 23×13.

$$
\begin{array}{r} 23 \\ \times\ 13 \end{array}
\longrightarrow
\begin{array}{r} 23 \\ \times\ 3 \\ \hline 69 \end{array}
+
\begin{array}{r} 23 \\ \times\ 10 \\ \hline 230 \end{array}
\longrightarrow
\begin{array}{r} 69 \\ +\ 230 \\ \hline 299 \end{array}
$$

$$23 \times 13 = 299$$

You can combine all of the steps into a single problem. As you multiply by each factor, record the products below one another. Be sure to write the digits in their place-value columns. Then add to find the final product.

Example Multiply 23×13.

$$
\begin{array}{r}
23 \\
\times\ 13 \\
\hline
69 \leftarrow (3 \times 23) \\
+230 \leftarrow (10 \times 23) \\
\hline
299
\end{array}
$$

PRACTICE

Find each product. In the first two problems, some of the work has been done; you need to add to find the final product.

1.
$$
\begin{array}{r} 11 \\ \times\ 13 \\ \hline 33 \\ +\ 110 \end{array}
\qquad
\begin{array}{r} 121 \\ \times\ 22 \\ \hline 242 \\ +\ 2{,}420 \end{array}
\qquad
\begin{array}{r} 302 \\ \times\ 13 \end{array}
\qquad
\begin{array}{r} 21 \\ \times\ 25 \end{array}
\qquad
\begin{array}{r} 43 \\ \times\ 21 \end{array}
$$

2.
$$
\begin{array}{r} 400 \\ \times\ 52 \end{array}
\qquad
\begin{array}{r} 610 \\ \times\ 15 \end{array}
\qquad
\begin{array}{r} 80 \\ \times\ 36 \end{array}
\qquad
\begin{array}{r} 63 \\ \times\ 31 \end{array}
\qquad
\begin{array}{r} 95 \\ \times\ 11 \end{array}
$$

Rewrite each problem in column form. Then find the product.

3. $231 \times 30 =$ _____

4. $32 \times 513 =$ _____

5. $30 \times 71 =$ _____

6. $302 \times 23 =$ _____

7. $44 \times 22 =$ _____

8. $50 \times 51 =$ _____

9. $22 \times 900 =$ _____

10. $16 \times 200 =$ _____

11. $860 \times 11 =$ _____

Estimating Products

To estimate a product, round the factors before you multiply.

- Round each factor to its greatest place value.
- Multiply the front-end digits.
- Write a zero in the product for each zero in the rounded factors.

Examples

Estimate 9 × 389.

$$\begin{array}{r} 389 \rightarrow 400 \\ \times\ 9 \quad\ \times\ 9^* \\ \hline 3,600 \end{array}$$

9 × 389 ≈ 3,600

Estimate 19 × 894.

$$\begin{array}{r} 894 \rightarrow 900 \\ \times\ 19 \rightarrow \times\ 20 \\ \hline 18,000 \end{array}$$

19 × 894 ≈ 18,000

Note: It is not necessary to round a one-digit factor.

PRACTICE

Use rounding to estimate each product. Remember, your estimate should have at least one zero for every zero in the rounded numbers.

1. $\begin{array}{r} 67 \\ \times\ 12 \\ \hline \end{array}$

2. $\begin{array}{r} 97 \\ \times\ 29 \\ \hline \end{array}$

3. $\begin{array}{r} 1,927 \\ \times\ 9 \\ \hline \end{array}$

4. $\begin{array}{r} \$29.00 \\ \times\ 3 \\ \hline \end{array}$

5. $\begin{array}{r} \$12.59 \\ \times\ 5 \\ \hline \end{array}$

6. $\begin{array}{r} 87 \text{ feet} \\ \times\ 18 \\ \hline \end{array}$

7. $\begin{array}{r} \$129 \\ \times\ 5 \\ \hline \end{array}$

8. $\begin{array}{r} 459 \\ \times\ 72 \\ \hline \end{array}$

9. 78 × 81 = _____

10. 603 × 92 = _____

11. 789 × 63 = _____

12. 92 × 37 = _____

Working with Word Problems

To solve a word problem, first read the problem to identify the question. Next, find out what information you have. Then make a plan to solve the problem. The following information can help you decide whether to add, subtract, multiply, or divide.

- Add to put together amounts that are different to find how many in all.

- Subtract to remove or take apart to find what is left.
  Subtract to compare to find the difference.

- Multiply to find how many in all when there are several of the same amount.

- Divide to separate into equal groups.

PRACTICE

Circle the letter of the best method to use to solve each problem. Be able to explain your choices. You do not have to find the answer.

1. There are 23 tables in the café. There are 4 seats at each table. How many seats in all are there at the café?

   A add
   B subtract
   C multiply

2. Amanda is covering a kitchen wall with square tiles. There will be 12 rows of tiles. Each row will have 24 tiles. How many tiles will she use in all?

   F add
   G subtract
   H multiply

3. Katherine bought 12 blouses. She got $12 off of the price of each blouse. How much money did she save?

   A add
   B subtract
   C multiply

4. Sangeeta is collecting toys for charity. She picked up 27 boxes of toys at the local high school. The Benefactor Club gave her another 25 boxes of toys. How many boxes does she have?

   F add
   G subtract
   H multiply

5. When Randy bought his puppy, it weighed 3 pounds. The puppy now weighs 14 pounds. How many pounds has the puppy gained?

   A add
   B subtract
   C multiply

6. Carmela bought five 12-ounce bags of walnuts. How many ounces of walnuts did she buy?

   F add
   G subtract
   H multiply

These word problems do not give enough information. Tell what additional information you need to solve each problem.

7. Rent City charges $21 a day to rent a small car, $29 a day for a midsize car, and $42 a day for a sedan. Eric rented a car for 3 days. How much did he owe?

   You need to know _____

   _____

8. The caterer at Jeanette's wedding charged $19 per person. What was the total charge?

   You also need to know _____

   _____

9. Carlos is building a brick patio. There will be 2 bricks per square foot of patio. How many bricks does Carlos need?

   You also need to know _____

   _____

Use this information to set up and solve Problems 10–13. Use estimation to check your work.

Julius is a telemarketer. He earns $4 for every sale he makes. This list shows how many sales Julius made each day last week.

Monday	32
Tuesday	27
Wednesday	10
Thursday	30
Friday	6

10. How much money did Julius make on Monday?

12. How many sales did Julius make in all last week?

11. How many more sales did Julius make on Monday than he made on Friday?

13. On average, Julius makes 21 sales a day. At that rate, about how many sales will he make in 22 workdays? (Estimate.)

Multiplication Skills Checkup

Circle the letter for the correct answer to each problem. Cross out unreasonable answers before you start to work on a problem.

1.
10
× 9

A   19
B   90
C   99
D   900
E   None of these

2.
78
× 3

F   224
G   234
H   254
J   2,324
K   None of these

3.
521
× 24

A   13,026
B   13,126
C   12,504
D   12,404
E   None of these

4.
39
× 5

F   195
G   155
H   185
J   355
K   None of these

5.
150
× 3

A   45
B   35
C   350
D   650
E   None of these

6.
240
× 32

F   120
G   768
H   668
J   7,248
K   None of these

7. There will be a total of 15 people at Marco's barbecue. He figures he needs 3 cans of soda for each person. How many cans of soda should Marco buy?

A 18   C 30
B 45   D 35

8. The butcher suggested that Marco buy 1 pound of steak for each person at the barbecue. The steak costs $5 per pound. How much will the steak cost?

F $20   H $55
G $ 7.50   J $75

9. Marco can buy German potato salad for $15. He can buy regular potato salad for $13.50. To find how much more the German potato salad costs than the regular potato salad, what should Marco do?

A add
B subtract
C multiply
D divide

10. Each week, Cindy drives 187 miles to get to and from work. About how many miles is that each month? (1 month = 4 weeks)

F   400
G   600
H   800
J   1,000

11.
$6 \times 92 =$

A 542
B 552
C 642
D 462
E None of these

12.
$61 \times 10 =$

F   71
G 610
H 6,100
J   61
K None of these

13.
$203 \times 4 =$

A 812
B 8,012
C 612
D 807
E None of these

14.
$\$21 \times 2 =$

F $23
G $420
H $41
J $42
K None of these

15.
$12 \times 243 =$

A 2,918
B 2,816
C 2,916
D 729
E None of these

16.
$850 \times 6 =$

F 5,200
G 4,830
H 4,700
J 5,100
K None of these

17. Which of the following, if any, equals 57?

A 57×0
B 57×1
C 57×57
D None of these

18. Which of the following problems, if any, can be solved with multiplication?

F Larry has $2,000 in his vacation fund. He spends $559 on plane tickets. How much is left?
G Clint buys a shirt for $52, a hat for $62.75, and shoes for $89. How much did he spend?
H Jorge buys 24 pears for 51 cents each. How much did he spend?
J None of these

19. Which of these, if any, has the same value as 41×3?

A $41 + 41 + 41$
B $41 \times 2 \times 1$
C $41 \times 3 \times 0$
D None of these

20. Which of these *does not* have the same value as 67×20?

F 20×67
G $67 \times 20 \times 1$
H $67 \times 4 \times 5$
J $67 \times 20 \times 0$

21. Which pair of factors has a product of about 16,000?

A 425×33
B 515×165
C 187×295
D 42×387

Division

Reviewing Basic Division Concepts

Division is the process of separating an amount into equal parts. You divide to find out how many equal groups can be made, or to find the number in each group.

- Questions often have words that signal division.

Examples

> The stack of books was *shared equally* among 4 people.
> How many *equal groups* of 3 can be made from 15?
> There are 15 chairs and 3 tables. Each table gets *the same*
> *number* of chairs. *How many* chairs *for each* table?

- The number being divided is called the **dividend**.

- The number you divide by is called the **divisor**.

- The answer is called the **quotient**.

- Division can be written two ways:
  - as a division **sentence** using the division symbol ÷
  - using a division **frame** $\overline{)}$

sentence

divisor
↓
$96 \div 3 = 32$
↑   ↑
dividend quotient

frame

32 ← quotient
$3\overline{)96}$ ← dividend
↑
divisor

- The order of the numbers in a division problem is important. $18 \div 3 \neq 3 \div 18$

- If you divide a number by 1, the value does not change. $125 \div 1 = 125$ $1\overline{)125}^{\,125}$

- If you divide any number except 0 by itself, quotient will be 1. $125 \div 125 = 1$ $125\overline{)125}^{\,1}$

- If you divide zero by any nonzero number, the quotient is zero. $0 \div 35 = 0$ $35\overline{)0}^{\,0}$

- Division and multiplication are opposites. For each division fact, there is another division fact, and there are two related multiplication facts.

  Division facts: $72 \div 8 = 9$ Related multiplication facts: $8 \times 9 = 72$
                  $72 \div 9 = 8$ $9 \times 8 = 72$

- You cannot divide any number by zero. Mathematicians say dividing by zero is undefined because you cannot find a related multiplication fact.

PRACTICE

Fill in the blanks.

1. $671 \div 1 =$ _____

2. $0 \div 89 =$ _____

3. $845 \div$ _____ $= 845$

4. $75 \div 5 = 15$, so $5 \times$ _____ $= 75$.

5. $81 \div \square$ is the same as $9\overline{)81}$. $\square =$ ___

6. $37 \div 37 =$ _____

Reviewing Basic Division Facts

To solve division problems quickly and efficiently, you need to know basic division facts. Because division and multiplication are related, you can use multiplication facts to help you with division.

Example $42 \div 7 = \square$

- Think of a related multiplication fact. $\square \times 7 = 42$
- Find the missing factor. $6 \times 7 = 42$, so $42 \div 7 = 6$

$$42 \div 7 = 6$$

PRACTICE

Find each quotient. Study any facts that you cannot recall quickly and accurately.

1. $12 \div 6 = \underline{\hspace{1cm}}$ $16 \div 4 = \underline{\hspace{1cm}}$ $8 \div 4 = \underline{\hspace{1cm}}$ $18 \div 6 = \underline{\hspace{1cm}}$

2. $6 \div 3 = \underline{\hspace{1cm}}$ $32 \div 4 = \underline{\hspace{1cm}}$ $36 \div 6 = \underline{\hspace{1cm}}$ $20 \div 4 = \underline{\hspace{1cm}}$

3. $30 \div 5 = \underline{\hspace{1cm}}$ $15 \div 3 = \underline{\hspace{1cm}}$ $9 \div 3 = \underline{\hspace{1cm}}$ $8 \div 2 = \underline{\hspace{1cm}}$

4. $10 \div 2 = \underline{\hspace{1cm}}$ $28 \div 4 = \underline{\hspace{1cm}}$ $10 \div 5 = \underline{\hspace{1cm}}$ $6 \div 2 = \underline{\hspace{1cm}}$

5. $12 \div 3 = \underline{\hspace{1cm}}$ $4 \div 2 = \underline{\hspace{1cm}}$ $21 \div 3 = \underline{\hspace{1cm}}$ $27 \div 3 = \underline{\hspace{1cm}}$

6. $49 \div 7 = \underline{\hspace{1cm}}$ $24 \div 3 = \underline{\hspace{1cm}}$ $42 \div 6 = \underline{\hspace{1cm}}$ $35 \div 5 = \underline{\hspace{1cm}}$

7. $45 \div 5 = \underline{\hspace{1cm}}$ $35 \div 7 = \underline{\hspace{1cm}}$ $14 \div 7 = \underline{\hspace{1cm}}$ $24 \div 6 = \underline{\hspace{1cm}}$

8. $16 \div 2 = \underline{\hspace{1cm}}$ $18 \div 2 = \underline{\hspace{1cm}}$ $40 \div 5 = \underline{\hspace{1cm}}$ $64 \div 8 = \underline{\hspace{1cm}}$

9. $36 \div 4 = \underline{\hspace{1cm}}$ $56 \div 8 = \underline{\hspace{1cm}}$ $25 \div 5 = \underline{\hspace{1cm}}$ $48 \div 8 = \underline{\hspace{1cm}}$

10. $63 \div 9 = \underline{\hspace{1cm}}$ $18 \div 3 = \underline{\hspace{1cm}}$ $81 \div 9 = \underline{\hspace{1cm}}$ $54 \div 9 = \underline{\hspace{1cm}}$

Using a Division Frame

When using a division frame $\overline{)}$, write the **dividend** (the number being divided) inside the frame. The **divisor** (the number you are dividing by) is placed at the left of the frame. The **quotient** (answer) is written above the frame.

Example $105 \div 5 = 21$ $5\overline{)\smash{105}}^{21}$

You can use multiplication to check your answer. Multiply the quotient by the divisor; the product should be equal to the dividend.

$$5\overline{)105}^{\,21}$$

Check
$$\begin{array}{r} 21 \\ \times\ 5 \\ \hline 105 \end{array}$$

PRACTICE

Rewrite Numbers 1–10 using a division frame.

1. $70 \div 5$

2. $98 \div 2$

3. $24 \div 12$

4. $142 \div 12$

5. What is 150 divided by 10?

6. What is 575 divided by 25?

7. What is ninety divided by fifteen?

8. What is eighty-one divided by nine?

9. What is 212 inches divided by 4?

10. What is 98 feet divided by 2?

For Numbers 11–16, write a division frame and fill in the dividend and the divisor. You do *not* have to solve the problems.

11. You must divide 16 tokens among 4 people. How many tokens will each person get?

12. After a meal, Lauren offered to pay the bill. She paid $20 for 5 hamburgers. How much did each hamburger cost?

13. Giles has a concert 1,200 miles away. He has three days to get there. If he divides the distance evenly, how many miles will he drive each day?

14. Rent is $654 per month. Three roommates share the cost evenly. How much does each one pay per month?

15. You used 12 gallons of gas during a 250-mile trip. How far did you drive on each gallon of gas?

16. Helena must knit 12 pairs of mittens before Christmas, which is 24 days away. On average, how many days does she have to knit each pair of mittens?

Dividing by a One-Digit Divisor

To divide the number in the frame, start on the left with the digit in the greatest place value. Work to the right.
- Divide one digit at a time.
- Write the quotient directly above the digit you are dividing.

Example Find 48 ÷ 2.

4 (tens) divided by 2 = 2 (tens)
8 (ones) divided by 2 = 4 (ones)

$$\begin{array}{r} 2\ 4 \\ 2\overline{)4\ 8} \end{array}$$

48 ÷ 2 = 24

Use multiplication to check your answer. When you multiply the quotient by the divisor, you should get the dividend.

$$\begin{array}{r} 2\ 4 \\ 2\overline{)48} \end{array} \qquad \begin{array}{r} 2\ 4 \longleftarrow \text{quotient} \\ \times\ 2 \longleftarrow \text{divisor} \\ \hline 4\ 8 \longleftarrow \text{dividend} \end{array}$$

PRACTICE

Find each quotient. If there is a dollar sign or a label in the dividend, be sure to include it in the quotient. Use multiplication to check your answers.

1. $4\overline{)84}$	4. $8\overline{)88 \text{ inches}}$	7. $2\overline{)448}$	10. $3\overline{)996}$
2. $3\overline{)96}$	5. $3\overline{)336}$	8. $3\overline{)\$396}$	11. $2\overline{)644}$
3. $2\overline{)268}$	6. $2\overline{)824}$	9. $4\overline{)484}$	12. $3\overline{)693}$

After you place the first digit in the quotient, you must write a digit above each remaining digit of the dividend, including the zeros. Remember that zero divided by any nonzero number is zero.

Examples

$$\begin{array}{r} 204 \\ 2\overline{)408} \end{array} \qquad \begin{array}{r} 130 \\ 3\overline{)390} \end{array}$$

PRACTICE

Find each quotient. Check your answers using multiplication.

13. 505 ÷ 5	15. 408 ÷ 2	17. 440 ÷ 4	19. 906 ÷ 3
14. 603 ÷ 3	16. 840 ÷ 4	18. 804 ÷ 2	20. 460 ÷ 2

Dividing by a One-Digit Divisor (continued)

If the first digit is less than the number you are dividing by, regroup.

• Combine the first two digits and divide the resulting two-digit number.

• Write the quotient above the second digit.

• Divide the next digit.

Examples   Find 368 ÷ 4.

$$\begin{array}{r} 92 \\ 4\overline{)368} \end{array}$$

The first digit, 3, is less than 4.
Combine 3 with the next digit, 6.
3 (hundreds) + 6 (tens) = 36 (tens)
36 (tens) ÷ 4 = 9 (tens)
Write 9 in the tens place above 6.

8 (ones) ÷ 4 = 2 (ones)
Write 2 in the ones place above 8.

$$368 ÷ 4 = 92$$

Find 205 ÷ 5.

$$\begin{array}{r} 41 \\ 5\overline{)205} \end{array}$$

The first digit, 2, is less than 5.
Combine 2 with the next digit, 0.
2 (hundreds) + 0 (tens) = 20 (tens)
20 (tens) ÷ 5 = 4 (tens)
Write 4 in the tens place above 0.

5 (ones) ÷ 5 = 1 (one)
Write 1 in the ones place above 5.

$$205 ÷ 5 = 41$$

PRACTICE

Find each quotient. Use multiplication to check your answers.

21. $3\overline{)246}$

24. $7\overline{)420}$

27. $5\overline{)255}$

30. $9\overline{)189}$

22. $8\overline{)328}$

25. $4\overline{)128}$

28. $8\overline{)640}$

31. $4\overline{)200}$

23. $7\overline{)560}$

26. $5\overline{)300}$

29. $9\overline{)369}$

32. $7\overline{)427}$

Finding a Remainder

Not all amounts can be evenly divided. For example, if you divide 9 objects into 2 equal groups, each group will have 4 objects and there will be 1 object left over. The leftover amount is called the **remainder**. In division, the remainder is written as part of the quotient as shown.

$$\begin{array}{r} 4\,R1 \\ 2\overline{)9} \end{array} \qquad 9 \div 2 = 4\,R1$$

When the number you are dividing cannot be evenly divided:
* List multiplication facts in which the divisor is one of the factors.
* Find the fact with a product that is *less than* the dividend, but is as close to the dividend as possible.

Example $3\overline{)17}$

$3 \times 1 = 3 \qquad 3 \times 2 = 6 \qquad 3 \times 3 = 9 \qquad 3 \times 4 = 12 \qquad 3 \times 5 = 15 \qquad 3 \times 6 = 18$

* Write the other factor for that fact in the quotient.
* Write the product below the dividend and then subtract to find the remainder.
* Write the remainder in the product.

Check your answer. Multiply the quotient by the divisor, and then add the remainder to the product. The result should match the dividend.

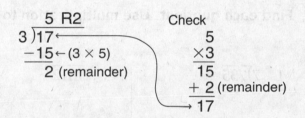

PRACTICE

Find each quotient. Make sure you write the remainder as part of the quotient. (*Hint*: The remainder must be smaller than the number you are dividing by.) Use multiplication to check your answers.

1. $3\overline{)8}$

2. $6\overline{)45}$

3. $9\overline{)73}$

4. $7\overline{)19}$

5. $5\overline{)27}$

6. $6\overline{)47}$

7. $4\overline{)18}$

8. $7\overline{)31}$

9. $6\overline{)56}$

10. $8\overline{)43}$

11. $9\overline{)50}$

12. $2\overline{)13}$

13. $37 \div 4 =$ _____

14. $52 \div 7 =$ _____

15. $67 \div 8 =$ _____

16. $85 \div 9 =$ _____

17. $57 \div 8 =$ _____

18. $36 \div 5 =$ _____

Regrouping After You Begin to Divide

Sometimes, after you place the first number in the quotient, the next digit to divide is less than the number you are dividing by. If that happens, write a zero in the answer above the digit. Then combine digits.

Example   Find 428 ÷ 4.

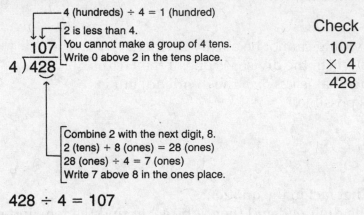

4 (hundreds) ÷ 4 = 1 (hundred)

2 is less than 4.
You cannot make a group of 4 tens.
Write 0 above 2 in the tens place.

$$107 \\ 4\overline{)428}$$

Check

$$\begin{array}{r} 107 \\ \times\ 4 \\ \hline 428 \end{array}$$

Combine 2 with the next digit, 8.
2 (tens) + 8 (ones) = 28 (ones)
28 (ones) ÷ 4 = 7 (ones)
Write 7 above 8 in the ones place.

428 ÷ 4 = 107

PRACTICE

Find each quotient. Use multiplication to check your answers.

1. 7)735

2. 9)981

3. 5)545

4. 6)624

5. 2)812

6. 4)812

7. 5)1,045

8. 9)927

9. 3)627

10. 8)840

11. 6)612

12. 9)945

13. 4)1,212

14. 3)2,709

15. 5)1,540

16. 6)1,230

Estimating Quotients for One-Digit Divisors

One way to estimate a quotient is to find the first digit of the quotient, and then write a zero for each remaining digit of the dividend. With this method, the estimate will always be less than the exact answer.

Example   Estimate $2,143 \div 5$.

$$\frac{400}{5 \overline{)2,143}}$$

Divide 21 (hundreds) by 5.
Write 4 (hundreds) in the quotient above 1.
Write zeros in the quotient above 4 and 3 of the dividend.

$$2,143 \div 5 \approx 400$$

PRACTICE

Estimate each quotient. After you write the first digit in the quotient, be sure to write a zero above each remaining digit of the dividend.

1. $3\overline{)1,267}$

2. $6\overline{)364}$

3. $7\overline{)816}$

4. $4\overline{)513}$

5. $4\overline{)1,091}$

6. $3\overline{)982}$

7. $2\overline{)564}$

8. $8\overline{)9,320}$

9. $4\overline{)890}$

10. $9\overline{)1,875}$

Circle the letter of the best estimate for each problem.

11. $3\overline{)628}$
   A 100
   B   20
   C 200
   D   10

12. $9\overline{)203}$
   F 100
   G   10
   H 200
   J   20

13. $9\overline{)7,218}$
   A 1,000
   B   800
   C   700
   D   500

14. $4\overline{)3,033}$
   F 700
   G less than 700
   H 800
   J more than 800

15. $8\overline{)806}$
   A 100
   B   10
   C more than 100
   D less than 100

Using Long Division

Completing a division problem can require several steps. **Long division** is a method of showing each step as you divide. Those steps are: divide, multiply, subtract, and bring down. You may need to repeat the steps, as shown.

Example   Find $72 \div 4$.

- **Divide** 7 (tens) $\div 4 = 1$ (ten). Write 1(ten) above the 7. $4\overline{)72}$ with 1 above

- **Multiply** 4×1 (ten) = 4 (tens) Write 4 below the 7. $\begin{array}{r} 1 \\ 4\overline{)72} \\ 4 \end{array}$

- **Subtract** 7 (tens) $- 4$ (tens) = 3 (tens) $\begin{array}{r} 1 \\ 4\overline{)72} \\ -4 \\ \hline 3 \end{array}$

- **Bring down** Bring down the next digit, 2. $\begin{array}{r} 1 \\ 4\overline{)72} \\ -4\downarrow \\ \hline 32 \end{array}$

- **Divide**   3 (tens) + 2 (ones) = 32 (ones)
              32 (ones) $\div 4 = 8$ (ones)
              Write 8 (ones) above the 2. $\begin{array}{r} 18 \\ 4\overline{)72} \\ -4\downarrow \\ \hline 32 \end{array}$

- **Multiply** 4×8 (ones) = 32 (ones)
              Write 32 below the 32.

- **Subtract** $32 - 32 = 0$ $\begin{array}{r} 18 \\ 4\overline{)72} \\ -4\downarrow \\ \hline 32 \\ -32 \\ \hline 0 \end{array}$

- **Bring down** There are no more digits to bring down.
              The division is complete.

        $72 \div 4 = 18$

PRACTICE

Find each quotient. Use long division and show your work for each step. Then multiply the quotient by the divisor to check your answer.

1. $3\overline{)75}$

2. $2\overline{)58}$

3. $5\overline{)65}$

4. $3\overline{)81}$

5. $7\overline{)84}$

6. $5\overline{)70}$

7. $6\overline{)84}$

8. $8\overline{)296}$

9. $5\overline{)260}$

10. $9\overline{)495}$

11. $272 \div 4 =$ _____

12. $672 \div 6 =$ _____

13. $575 \div 5 =$ _____

14. $917 \div 7 =$ _____

15. $434 \div 7 =$ _____

Dividing Greater Amounts

Follow the steps for long division when dividing greater numbers. You may need to repeat the steps to complete the problem.

Example   Find $138 \div 4$.

$$\begin{array}{r} 3 \\ 4\overline{)138} \end{array}$$

• **Divide**   13 (tens) $\div$ 4 = 3 (tens). Write 3 above the 3 of 13.

• **Multiply** 4×3 (tens) = 12 (tens). Write 12 below the 13.

$$\begin{array}{r} 3 \\ 4\overline{)138} \\ 12 \end{array}$$

• **Subtract**   13 (tens) – 12 (tens) = 1 (ten)

$$\begin{array}{r} 3 \\ 4\overline{)138} \\ -12 \\ \hline 1 \end{array}$$

• **Bring down**   Bring down the next digit, 8.

$$\begin{array}{r} 3 \\ 4\overline{)138} \\ -12\downarrow \\ \hline 18 \end{array}$$

• **Divide**   1 (ten) + 8 (ones) = 18 (ones)
  18 (ones) $\div$ 4 = 4 (ones)
  Write 4 above the 8.

$$\begin{array}{r} 34 \\ 4\overline{)138} \\ -12\downarrow \\ \hline 18 \end{array}$$

• **Multiply** 4×4 (ones) = 16 (ones)
  Write 16 below the 18.

$$\begin{array}{r} 34 \\ 4\overline{)138} \\ -12\downarrow \\ \hline 18 \\ 16 \end{array}$$

• **Subtract**   18 – 16 = 2

• **Bring down**   There are no more digits to bring down.
  There is a remainder of 2.
  Write R2 in the quotient.

$$\begin{array}{r} 34\ \text{R2} \\ 4\overline{)138} \\ -12\downarrow \\ \hline 18 \\ -16 \\ \hline 2 \end{array}$$

$138 \div 4 = 34$ R2

PRACTICE

Find each quotient. Check your answers.

1. $4\overline{)540}$

2. $8\overline{)176}$

3. $5\overline{)720}$

4. $9\overline{)198}$

5. $3\overline{)5,344}$

6. $2\overline{)3,305}$

7. $8\overline{)6,208}$

8. $6\overline{)4,503}$

9. $4\overline{)4,124}$

10. $5\overline{)9,375}$

11. $9\overline{)4,528}$

12. $7\overline{)4,872}$

Dividing by a Two-Digit Divisor

You will need to use at least the first 2 digits of the dividend to divide by a two-digit divisor. Combine digits to start dividing.

Example   Find 315 ÷ 15.

$$\overset{2}{15\overline{)315}}$$
⤴ Combine the first two digits.
3 (hundreds) + 1 (ten) = 31 (tens)
31 (tens) ÷ 15 = 2 (tens)
Write 2 above the 1 of 31.

$$\begin{array}{r} 21 \\ 15\overline{)315} \\ -30\!\downarrow \\ \hline 15 \\ -15 \\ \hline 0 \end{array}$$
Continue to follow the steps for long division to find the quotient.

315 ÷ 15 = 21

If the value of the first two digits of the dividend is less than the divisor, you will need to use the first *three* digits. Write the answer above the third digit.

Example   Find 217 ÷ 25.

$$\overset{8}{25\overline{)217}}$$
⤴ Combine the first two digits.
21 is less than 25. Use all three digits.
217 (ones) ÷ 25 = 8 (ones)
Write 8 (ones) in the ones column above the 7.

$$\begin{array}{r} 8\ \text{R}17 \\ 25\overline{)217} \\ -200 \\ \hline 17 \end{array}$$
Continue to follow the steps for long division to find the quotient.

217 ÷ 25 = 8 R17

PRACTICE

Find each quotient. Use multiplication to check your answers.

1. 15)30

2. 22)66

3. 12)168

4. 21)651

5. 15)450

6. 20)100

7. 30)120

8. 70)357

9. 25)158

10. 25)1,580

11. 12)185

12. 50)307

13. 82)328

14. 45)210

15. 50)2,540

16. 60)3,304

Working with Word Problems

To solve a word problem, start by reading the problem to identify the question. Next, find out what information you have. Then decide whether to add, subtract, multiply, or divide.

- Add to put together amounts that are different to find how many in all.
- Subtract to remove or take apart and find what is left.
  Subtract to compare or find the difference.
- Multiply to find how many in all when there are several of the same amount.
- Divide to separate into equal groups.

PRACTICE

Use the following information to answer Questions 1–4. Circle the letter of the best method to use to solve each problem. Be able to explain your choices. You do not have to find the answers.

> Luisa is running the art booth at the Children's Fair.
> This year the children are painting T-shirts.
> Luisa has 250 T-shirts and 5 boxes of fabric paint.

1. Each box of fabric paint contains 25 tubes of paint. How many tubes of paint does Luisa have in all?

   A add   C subtract
   B multiply   D divide

2. Luisa paid a total of $60 for the fabric paint. If the price of each box was the same, what was the cost of each box?

   F add   H subtract
   G multiply   J divide

3. The art booth will be open for 4 hours. Luisa wants to have an equal number of T-shirts ready to paint each hour. How many T-shirts should she set aside for each hour?

   A add   C subtract
   B multiply   D divide

4. At the end of the fair, 27 T-shirts are left. How many T-shirts were used?

   F add   H subtract
   G multiply   J divide

These word problems do not give enough information. Tell what information you need to know to solve the problem.

5. There are 31 days in March. About how much did the Suarez family pay per day for their cable service in March?

   _____

   _____

6. Roy is sorting widgets into 4 equal groups. How many widgets should there be in each group?

   _____

   _____

Working with Two-Step Word Problems

Many times, solving a problem involves more than just adding *or* subtracting *or* multiplying *or* dividing. You may need to add and then divide, or subtract and then multiply, and so on.

Example   Darren has three 6-packs of soda plus 2 extra cans. How many cans of soda does he have in all?

- Multiply to find the number of cans of soda in three 6-packs. $3 \times 6 = 18$
- Add on the extra cans. $18 + 2 = 20$

     Darren has 20 cans of soda.

PRACTICE

Circle the letter of the choice that correctly describes how to solve the problem.

1. Ben gets three 20-dollar bills from the ATM. He spends $12 of that money. How much money does he have left?

   A Subtract $12 from $20. Then multiply by 3.
   B Multiply $20 by 3. Then subtract $12.
   C Multiply $12 by 3. Then subtract $20.

2. Clarice bought 15 cookies. She gave 3 cookies to her husband. The rest were shared by her 4 children. How many cookies did each child get?

   F Add 3 to 15. Then divide by 4.
   G Subtract 4 from 15. Then divide by 3.
   H Subtract 3 from 15. Then divide by 4.

3. Howard must drive 360 miles for a meeting. He will be able to drive 60 miles an hour the entire way, but he plans to stop for an hour to have lunch with a friend. How long will the trip take?

   A Add 360 and 60. Then add 1.
   B Multiply 360 by 60. Then subtract 1.
   C Divide 360 by 60. Then add 1.

4. Gail bought a couch for $940. She put down a deposit of $100 and paid the balance in 24 equal payments. How much was each payment?

   F Subtract $100 from $940. Then divide by 24.
   G Divide $940 by 24. Then add $100.
   H Subtract $100 from $940. Then multiply by 24.

5. Mrs. Obama bought 4 pairs of socks at $2.29 per pair. With tax, the total was $9.89. How much was the tax?

   A Subtract $2.29 from $9.89. Then divide by 4.
   B Multiply $2.29 by 4. Then subtract from $9.89.
   C Add $2.29 to $9.89. Then divide by 4.

6. Hiro had $100. He spent $35 for a sweater and $19.89 for a shirt. How much money does he have left?

   F Subtract $19.89 from $35. Then subtract from $100.
   G Add $19.89 to $35. Then subtract from $100.
   H Subtract $35 from $100. Then add $19.89.

Division Skills Checkup

Circle the letter for the best answer to each problem. Try crossing out unreasonable answers before you start to work on each problem.

1. 7)294

   A 40 R4
   B 42
   C 40 R2
   D 32
   E None of these

2. 6,000 ÷ 4 =

   F 150
   G 1,200
   H 1,400
   J 1,500
   K None of these

3. 16 ÷ 3 =

   A 5
   B 6 R1
   C 6
   D 5 R1
   E None of these

4. 3)9,021

   F 37
   G 307
   H 3,007
   J 3,070
   K None of these

5. 4)96

   A 24
   B 22 R1
   C 14
   D 44 R1
   E None of these

6. How many cards will be left over if a deck of 52 cards is divided equally among 6 people?

   F 0   H 4
   G 2   J 6

7. Joe had programs printed for the community play. He paid $50 for 600 programs. How many programs did he get for each dollar spent?

   A 12   C 60
   B 83   D 50

8. The programs came packaged in 4 boxes. How many programs were in each box?

   F 100   H 150
   G 125   J 200

9. Play tickets cost $8.50 each. Mr. Izzarary bought 5 tickets and paid with a $50 bill. How much change should he receive?

   A $6.50   C $8
   B $8.50   D $7.50

10. The Seniors Club got a senior discount and paid only $7 a ticket. Each member of the club bought a ticket. The total cost was $105. How many tickets did the Seniors Club buy?

    F 18   H 12
    G 15   J 10

Division Skills Checkup (continued)

11. $5\overline{)8}$

   A 1
   B 2
   C 1 R2
   D 1 R3
   E None of these

12. $97 \div 10 =$

   F 97
   G 9 R7
   H 90 R7
   J 91
   K None of these

13. $33 \div 3 =$

   A 10
   B 11
   C 12
   D 10 R3
   E None of these

14. $306 \div 30 =$

   F 12
   G 102
   H 101
   J 192
   K None of these

15. $20\overline{)184}$

   A 900
   B 90
   C 9 R4
   D 90 R4
   E None of these

16. The Crow Theater has 1,512 seats. If there are 36 seats in each row, how many rows are there in the theater?

   F 42   H 48
   G 46   J 50

17. Which of these, if any, has the same value as $95 \div 5$?

   A $5 \div 95$
   B $95\overline{)5}$
   C $5\overline{)95}$
   D None of these

18. What sign goes in the box to make the second number sentence true?

$$78 \div 2 = 39$$
$$39 \boxed{} 2 = 78$$

   F $\div$
   G $\times$
   H $+$
   J $-$

19. Which of these number sentences is false?

   A $84 \div 1 = 84$
   B $57 \div 57 = 1$
   C $0 \div 12 = 0$
   D $1 \div 22 = 22$

20. Which is the best estimate of the quotient for $6,275 \div 60$?

   F 10
   G 100
   H 1,000
   J 10,000

Fractions

Reading and Writing Fractions

A fraction is a number that names a value less than 1. A fraction is written with one number above another and a bar in between them.

- The **denominator** is the number below the bar.
  It tells how many equal parts there are in 1 whole.

- The **numerator** is the number above the bar.
  It tells how many of the equal parts are described.

$$\frac{\text{numerator} \quad \rightarrow \quad \text{equal parts described}}{\text{denominator} \quad \rightarrow \quad \text{equal parts in one whole}}$$

Examples

What fraction of the cupcakes are chocolate?

6 equal cupcakes—the denominator is 6
5 of the cupcakes are chocolate—the numerator is 5

$\frac{5}{6}$ of the cupcakes are chocolate.

What fraction of the circle is shaded?

3 equal sections—the denominator is 3
2 of the sections are shaded—the numerator is 2

$\frac{2}{3}$ of the circle is shaded.

- As the number of equal parts increases (becomes greater):
  - the number in the denominator becomes greater
  - the size of each part decreases (gets smaller)

$\frac{1}{2}$ $\frac{1}{3}$ $\frac{1}{4}$ $\frac{1}{5}$ $\frac{1}{6}$

- A **proper fraction** names an amount less than 1.
  In a proper fraction, the number in the numerator is less than the number in the denominator. $\frac{1}{2}$, $\frac{6}{8}$, and $\frac{2}{3}$ are examples of proper fractions.

- When the number in the numerator is the same as the number in the denominator, the whole amount is named. This type of fraction is a **name for 1**.

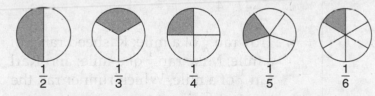

$\frac{4}{4} = 1$ $\frac{8}{8} = 1$ $\frac{12}{12} = 1$

Reading and Writing Fractions (continued)

- An **improper fraction** names an amount greater than 1. In an improper fraction, the numerator is greater than the denominator.

- A **mixed number** is a whole number together with a fraction. An improper fraction can be renamed as a mixed number.

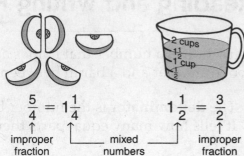

$$\frac{5}{4} = 1\frac{1}{4} \qquad 1\frac{1}{2} = \frac{3}{2}$$

improper   mixed   improper
fraction   numbers   fraction

PRACTICE

Circle the letter of the correct answer.

1. Craig filled his car with 15 gallons of gas. His wife drove the car and used 7 gallons of the gas. What fraction of the gas did she use?

   A $\frac{7}{15}$ C $\frac{8}{15}$

   B $\frac{15}{7}$ D $\frac{15}{8}$

2. Which fraction names the total amount shaded?

   F $\frac{3}{5}$ H $\frac{2}{5}$

   G $\frac{4}{5}$ J $\frac{6}{5}$

3. Which pair shows $\frac{10}{7}$ of the total amount shaded?

   A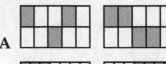

   B

   C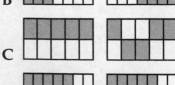

   D

4. Bernice cut 2 sandwiches into fourths. She ate 1 of the fourths. Which of these names the amount *not* eaten as a mixed number and as an improper fraction?

   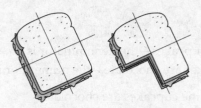

   F $\frac{5}{4}$; $1\frac{1}{4}$ H $\frac{7}{4}$; $1\frac{3}{4}$

   G $\frac{6}{4}$; $1\frac{2}{4}$ J $\frac{4}{4}$; 1

5. Troy ran $\frac{1}{8}$ of a mile; Rasheed ran $\frac{1}{4}$ of a mile; Mike ran $\frac{1}{5}$ of a mile; and Karl ran $\frac{1}{3}$ of a mile. Which runner ran the greatest distance?

   A Troy   C Rasheed
   B Mike   D Karl

6. Bonita's recipe calls for $1\frac{2}{3}$ cups of flour. She has a $\frac{1}{3}$-cup measure. How many times will she have to fill the $\frac{1}{3}$-cup measure?

   F 6   H 5
   G 4   J 3

Finding Equivalent Fractions

Equivalent fractions are fractions that are equal in value but have different numerators and denominators.

You can rename a fraction to an equivalent fraction in **higher terms**. Each part will get smaller and there will be more of them, so the numbers in the numerator and the denominator will increase (get higher). To rename to higher terms, **multiply** both the numerator and the denominator by the same number.

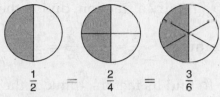

$$\frac{1}{2} = \frac{2}{4} = \frac{3}{6}$$

Examples

$$\frac{2}{3} = \frac{2 \times 2}{2 \times 3} = \frac{4}{6} \qquad \frac{2}{3} = \frac{3 \times 2}{3 \times 3} = \frac{6}{9} \qquad \frac{2}{3} = \frac{4 \times 2}{4 \times 3} = \frac{8}{12} \qquad \frac{2}{3} = \frac{4}{6} = \frac{6}{9} = \frac{8}{12}$$

PRACTICE

Fill in the boxes to rename each fraction to an equivalent fraction in higher terms.

1. $\dfrac{3}{5} = \dfrac{4 \times 3}{\square \times 5} = \dfrac{12}{\square}$

3. $\dfrac{4}{5} = \dfrac{3 \times 4}{\square \times 5} = \dfrac{\square}{\square}$

5. $\dfrac{3}{4} = \dfrac{\square}{12}$

7. $\dfrac{1}{8} = \dfrac{3}{\square}$

2. $\dfrac{4}{7} = \dfrac{\square \times 4}{2 \times 7} = \dfrac{\square}{14}$

4. $\dfrac{1}{6} = \dfrac{5 \times \square}{5 \times \square} = \dfrac{\square}{\square}$

6. $\dfrac{2}{5} = \dfrac{4}{\square}$

8. $\dfrac{1}{3} = \dfrac{\square}{15}$

You can also rename to an equivalent fraction in **lower terms**. The numbers are decreased (lowered) to simpler numbers, so this is often called **reducing** or **simplifying** the fraction. To rename to lower terms, divide both the numerator and the denominator by the same number.

Examples

$$\frac{20}{25} = \frac{20 \div 5}{25 \div 5} = \frac{4}{5} \qquad \frac{12}{15} = \frac{12 \div 3}{15 \div 3} = \frac{4}{5} \qquad \frac{8}{10} = \frac{8 \div 2}{10 \div 2} = \frac{4}{5} \qquad \frac{20}{25} = \frac{12}{15} = \frac{8}{10} = \frac{4}{5}$$

When the only number that will evenly divide the numerator and denominator is 1, the fraction is in its **simplest terms** or **lowest terms**.

PRACTICE

Fill in the boxes to rename each fraction to an equivalent fraction in lower terms.

9. $\dfrac{12}{14} = \dfrac{12 \div 2}{14 \div \square} = \dfrac{6}{\square}$

11. $\dfrac{8}{12} = \dfrac{8 \div 4}{\square \div 4} = \dfrac{\square}{\square}$

13. $\dfrac{14}{18} = \dfrac{\square}{9}$

15. $\dfrac{4}{18} = \dfrac{2}{\square}$

10. $\dfrac{5}{15} = \dfrac{5 \div 5}{15 \div \square} = \dfrac{1}{\square}$

12. $\dfrac{10}{12} = \dfrac{10 \div \square}{12 \div \square} = \dfrac{5}{\square}$

14. $\dfrac{20}{50} = \dfrac{4}{\square}$

16. $\dfrac{3}{6} = \dfrac{\square}{2}$

Finding Factors to Simplify Fractions

To simplify a fraction, divide the numerator and denominator by the same **factor**.

Example $\frac{3}{15} = \frac{3 \div 3}{15 \div 3} = \frac{1}{5}$

- To find its factors, think of the number as a product. List pairs of factors that have that product. Work in order to find all of the factors. Start with 1 times the number. Then try 2 times the number, 3 times the number, and so on. List only pairs that have the product you are looking for. When you come to a pair that is already listed, you can stop.

Example Find the factors of 24.

$1 \times 24 \qquad 2 \times 12 \qquad 3 \times 8 \qquad 4 \times 6 \qquad 6 \times 4$ is the same as 4×6—stop
The factors of 24 are 1, 2, 3, 4, 6, 8, 12, and 24.

- A number can be evenly divided by any of its factors. That means 24 can be evenly divided by 1, by 2, by 3, by 4, by 6, by 8, by 12, and by 24.

- Every whole number except 1 has at least 2 factors. Most numbers have more than 2 factors.

Examples

Number	Pairs of Factors for the Number	List of Factors for the Number
2	1×2	1, 2
3	1×3	1, 3
4	$1 \times 4, 2 \times 2$	1, 2, 4
5	1×5	1, 5
6	$1 \times 6, 2 \times 3$	1, 2, 3, 6

PRACTICE

Write all the pairs of factors for the number. Then list the factors in order from least to greatest.

Number	Pairs of Factors for the Number	List of Factors for the Number
10		
12		
15		
16		
18		
20		

Simplify each fraction. Look for factors to divide by in the tables above. *Remember:* In simplest terms, the only factor that will evenly divide both numerator and denominator is 1.

1. $\frac{8}{24} =$ 3. $\frac{16}{20} =$ 5. $\frac{6}{18} =$ 7. $\frac{6}{15} =$

2. $\frac{12}{18} =$ 4. $\frac{5}{15} =$ 6. $\frac{4}{24} =$ 8. $\frac{18}{24} =$

Renaming Whole Numbers to Fractions

Finding Names for One

The number 1 can be renamed as a fraction for any fractional unit. In a name for one, the number in the numerator is the same as the number in the denominator.

Examples $1 = \frac{3}{3}$ $\quad$ $1 = \frac{5}{5}$ $\quad$ $1 = \frac{100}{100}$

PRACTICE

Write the missing number to complete each name for one.

1. $1 = \dfrac{3}{\square}$

2. $1 = \dfrac{\square}{8}$

3. $1 = \dfrac{10}{\square}$

4. $1 = \dfrac{\square}{7}$

5. $\dfrac{\square}{} = \dfrac{6}{6}$

6. $1 = \dfrac{12}{\square}$

7. Ramona baked 24 cupcakes and then frosted all of them. What fraction of the cupcakes did she frost?

   F $\dfrac{24}{1}$ $\qquad$ H $\dfrac{1}{24}$

   G $\dfrac{24}{24}$ $\qquad$ J $\dfrac{12}{24}$

Renaming Whole Numbers Greater than One

You can rename a whole number greater than one as an improper fraction.

Example $\quad 2 = \dfrac{\square}{3}$

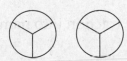

$2 = 1 + 1 = \frac{3}{3} + \frac{3}{3} = \frac{6}{3}$

$2 = \dfrac{6}{3}$

Shortcut:

- Multiply the whole number by the denominator of the fraction.
  $3 \times 2 = 6$

- Write the product as the numerator of the fraction.

- The denominator stays the same. $\quad 2 = \dfrac{6}{3}$

PRACTICE

Fill in the numerator to rename each whole number as an improper fraction.

8. $4 = \dfrac{\square}{3}$

9. $2 = \dfrac{\square}{5}$

10. $3 = \dfrac{\square}{9}$

11. $5 = \dfrac{\square}{2}$

12. $2 = \dfrac{\square}{8}$

13. $4 = \dfrac{\square}{5}$

14. Max had two 30-inch boards. He cut each board into 5 equal pieces. Which fraction correctly describes the result?

    F $\dfrac{5}{2}$ $\qquad$ H $\dfrac{10}{2}$

    G $\dfrac{10}{5}$ $\qquad$ J $\dfrac{10}{2}$

Renaming Improper Fractions and Mixed Numbers

To change a mixed number to an improper fraction, first change the whole number to a fraction with a denominator that matches the denominator of the fraction in the mixed number. Then add the numerators.

Example $2\frac{2}{3} = \frac{\square}{3}$

- Write the whole number as a fraction with a denominator of 3.

$$2 = 1 + 1 = \frac{3}{3} + \frac{3}{3} = \frac{6}{3}$$

- Add the renamed whole number and the fraction. Do not simplify.

$$2\frac{2}{3} = \frac{6}{3} + \frac{2}{3} = \frac{8}{3}$$

$$2\frac{2}{3} = \frac{8}{3}$$

Shortcut:

- Multiply the whole number by the denominator of the fraction. $3 \times 2 = 6$

$2\frac{2}{3}$

- Add the product to the numerator of the fraction. $6 + 2 = 8$

- Write the sum, 8, as the numerator for the improper fraction. The denominator, 3, remains the same. $\frac{8}{3}$

PRACTICE

Fill in the numerator to rename the mixed number as an improper fraction.

1. $1\frac{1}{4} = \frac{\square}{4}$

2. $1\frac{1}{5} = \frac{\square}{5}$

3. $3\frac{1}{7} = \frac{\square}{7}$

4. $2\frac{2}{9} = \frac{\square}{9}$

To change an improper fraction to a mixed number, you separate the fraction into names for 1. Use the denominator to decide which name for 1 you will use.

Example $\frac{11}{5} = \square$

- The denominator is 5. Separate $\frac{11}{5}$ into groups of $\frac{5}{5}$.

$$\frac{11}{5} = \frac{5}{5} + \frac{5}{5} + \frac{1}{5}$$

$$\frac{11}{5} = 1 + 1 + \frac{1}{5} = 2\frac{1}{5}$$

$$\frac{11}{5} = 2\frac{1}{5}$$

Shortcut:

- Divide the numerator by the denominator. $\frac{11}{5} = 11 \div 5 = 2\,R1$

- The whole number of the mixed number is 2. Write the remainder as the numerator of the fraction. The denominator, 5, remains the same. $2\,R1 = 2\frac{1}{5}$

PRACTICE

Rename each improper fraction as a whole number or a mixed number.

5. $\frac{16}{8} =$

6. $\frac{9}{8} =$

7. $\frac{8}{5} =$

8. $\frac{17}{5} =$

Comparing Fractions

When you compare fractions, first compare denominators. Then compare numerators.

- Denominators are the same, numerators are different

Example   Compare $\frac{4}{7}$ and $\frac{3}{7}$.

When denominators are the same, the fraction with the greater number in the numerator is greater.

$$\frac{4}{7} > \frac{3}{7}$$

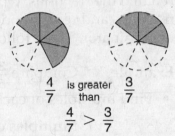

$\frac{4}{7}$ is greater than $\frac{3}{7}$

$$\frac{4}{7} > \frac{3}{7}$$

- Numerators are the same, denominators are different

Example   Compare $\frac{2}{8}$ and $\frac{2}{4}$.

When the numerators are the same, the fraction with the lower number in the denominator is greater.

$$\frac{2}{8} < \frac{2}{4}$$

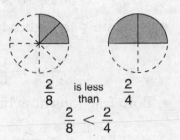

$\frac{2}{8}$ is less than $\frac{2}{4}$

$$\frac{2}{8} < \frac{2}{4}$$

PRACTICE

Write <, >, or = between the fractions in each pair.

1. $\frac{3}{7}$ $\frac{3}{10}$

2. $\frac{5}{12}$ $\frac{8}{12}$

3. $\frac{2}{15}$ $\frac{2}{20}$

4. $1\frac{5}{10}$ $1\frac{6}{10}$

Arrange these fractions in order from least to greatest.

5. $\frac{4}{5}$ $\frac{7}{5}$ $\frac{2}{5}$ $\frac{5}{5}$ _____

6. $\frac{1}{2}$ $\frac{1}{4}$ $\frac{1}{5}$ $\frac{1}{3}$ _____

7. $1\frac{1}{2}$ $1\frac{1}{3}$ $1\frac{1}{5}$ _____

Find the answer for each question.

8. Graham donated $\frac{3}{5}$ of his CD collection to the church rummage sale. Reggie donated $\frac{3}{7}$ of his CD collection. Who gave away a greater fraction of his CD collection?

_____

9. Marcy ran $\frac{7}{10}$ of a mile on Monday. On Wednesday she ran $\frac{5}{10}$ of a mile. On Friday she ran $\frac{9}{10}$ of a mile. On which day did she run the least distance?

_____

10. Ahmed correctly answered $\frac{12}{18}$ of the questions on the quiz. Hank correctly answered $\frac{10}{18}$ of the questions. Who correctly answered a greater number of questions?

_____

Comparing Fractions (continued)

To compare fractions when *neither* the numerators *nor* the denominators are the same, rename the fractions. One method is to find a denominator that is a multiple of both fractions and rename one (or both) of the fractions to an equivalent fraction with that denominator. Then, follow the method for comparing fractions with the same denominator.

Example   Compare $\frac{3}{5}$ and $\frac{7}{10}$.

- Find multiples of each denominator.

    Multiples of 5:   5, 10, 15, 20, 25…
    Multiples of 10: 10, 20, 30,…

    Since **10** is a multiple of both numbers, you can use **10** as the denominator.

- Rename $\frac{3}{5}$ to higher terms as tenths.

$$\frac{2 \times 3}{2 \times 5} = \frac{6}{10}$$

- Both fractions now have a denominator of tenths. Compare numerators.

$$\frac{6}{10} < \frac{7}{10} \quad \text{so} \quad \frac{3}{5} < \frac{7}{10}$$

PRACTICE

List multiples of both denominators for each pair of fractions. Circle a multiple in both lists and write both fractions with the same denominator. Finally, write <, >, or = between the original pair of fractions.

11. $\frac{2}{4}$ $\frac{4}{6}$ multiples of 4 _____

                            multiples of 6 _____

12. $\frac{3}{4}$ $\frac{9}{12}$ multiples of 4 _____

                            multiples of 12 _____

13. $\frac{1}{2}$ $\frac{3}{5}$ multiples of 2 _____

                            multiples of 5 _____

Compare. Write <, >, or =.

14. $\frac{7}{8}$ $\frac{23}{24}$ 16. $\frac{3}{4}$ $\frac{7}{16}$ 18. $\frac{9}{12}$ $\frac{5}{8}$

15. $\frac{2}{9}$ $\frac{6}{27}$ 17. $\frac{8}{15}$ $\frac{13}{30}$ 19. $\frac{6}{7}$ $\frac{9}{10}$

Adding and Subtracting Like Fractions

The denominators of fractions tell you what you are adding or subtracting. Instead of apples or boxes, you are adding or subtracting thirds or fifths, and so on.

When the fractions have **like denominators** (the same denominator), write that denominator in the answer. Then add (or subtract) the numerators. If possible, rename the answer to simplest terms.

Examples

Find $\frac{5}{8} + \frac{5}{8}$.

5 eighths + 5 eighths = 10 eighths

$$\frac{5}{8} + \frac{5}{8} = \frac{10}{8} = 1\frac{1}{4}$$

$$\frac{5}{8} + \frac{5}{8} = 1\frac{1}{4}$$

Find $\frac{5}{5} - \frac{3}{5}$.

5 fifths − 3 fifths = 2 fifths

$$\frac{5}{5} - \frac{3}{5} = \frac{2}{5}$$

PRACTICE

Find each sum or difference. Write the answer in simplest terms.

1. $\frac{1}{6} + \frac{4}{6} =$

2. $\frac{9}{10} - \frac{4}{10} =$

3. $\frac{7}{10} + \frac{5}{10} =$

4. $\frac{7}{12} - \frac{5}{12} =$

5. $\frac{5}{7} + \frac{3}{7} =$

6. $\frac{7}{9} + \frac{7}{9} =$

7. $\frac{4}{9} + \frac{1}{9} =$

8. $\frac{15}{16} - \frac{7}{16} =$

9. $\frac{8}{15} - \frac{7}{15} =$

10. $\frac{1}{6} + \frac{2}{6} =$

11. $\frac{7}{10} + \frac{3}{10} =$

12. $\frac{9}{10} - \frac{1}{10} =$

13. $\frac{3}{8} + \frac{2}{8} =$

14. $\frac{7}{10} - \frac{3}{10} =$

15. $\frac{6}{13} - \frac{6}{13} =$

16. $\frac{4}{5} + \frac{3}{5} =$

17. $\frac{7}{15} - \frac{2}{15} =$

18. $\frac{3}{8} + \frac{5}{8} =$

Multiplying Fractions

In math, the word *of* means multiply.

Suppose you had \$10, and you spent $\frac{3}{5}$ of the money. How much would you have spent? One way to find out is to divide \$10 into 5 equal parts and then take 3 of those 5 equal parts. Or, you could multiply: $\frac{3}{5}$ of 10 means $\frac{3}{5} \times 10$.

Example Find $\frac{2}{3} \times \frac{3}{8}$.

- Multiply the numbers in the numerators.
- Then multiply the numbers in the denominators. If possible, simplify to lowest terms.

$$\frac{2}{3} \times \frac{3}{8} = \frac{1}{4}$$

$$\text{multiply} \longrightarrow \frac{2}{3} \times \frac{3}{8} = \frac{2 \times 3}{3 \times 8} = \frac{6}{24}$$
$$\text{multiply} \longrightarrow$$

$$\frac{6}{24} = \frac{6 \div 6}{24 \div 6} = \frac{1}{4}$$

To multiply a whole number by a fraction, write the whole number as a fraction.

Example Find $\frac{3}{5} \times 10$.

- Write the whole number in the numerator and write 1 in the denominator.
- Then multiply numerators and denominators.

$$\frac{3}{5} \times 10 = 6$$

$$\frac{3}{5} \times 10 = \frac{3}{5} \times \frac{10}{1} = \frac{30}{5} = 6$$

$$\frac{3}{5} \times 10 = 6$$

PRACTICE

Find each product. Write answers in simplest terms.

1. $\frac{2}{3} \times \frac{1}{4} =$

2. $\frac{5}{7} \times \frac{1}{3} =$

3. $3 \times \frac{1}{3} =$

4. $\frac{1}{2}$ of $\frac{1}{4} =$

5. $\frac{1}{2} \times \frac{1}{2} \times \frac{1}{3} =$

6. $\frac{3}{7} \times 35 =$

7. $25 \times \frac{1}{5} =$

8. $\frac{3}{8} \times \frac{3}{8} =$

9. $\frac{1}{3}$ of $15 =$

10. $\frac{3}{4} \times \frac{2}{3} \times \frac{1}{2} =$

11. $\frac{3}{4} \times \frac{1}{5} =$

12. $\frac{1}{6} \times \frac{1}{4} =$

13. $\frac{1}{2} \times \frac{1}{3} =$

14. $\frac{1}{5}$ of $\frac{1}{2} =$

15. $\frac{1}{2} \times \frac{1}{4} \times 8 =$

16. $\frac{1}{7} \times \frac{1}{2} =$

17. $\frac{1}{4} \times \frac{1}{3} =$

18. $\frac{1}{2} \times 16 =$

19. $\frac{2}{3}$ of $6 =$

20. $\frac{2}{7}$ of $49 =$

Canceling Fractions Before Multiplying

You can simplify fractions *before* you multiply rather than after. This is called **canceling**.

Example   Find $\frac{2}{3} \times \frac{3}{5}$.

- Look for the same factor in the numerator and the denominator.
- Divide. Cross out the original numbers and record the quotients.
- Multiply. Use the numbers that result from canceling to multiply.

$$\frac{2}{3} \times \frac{3}{5} = \frac{2 \times \overset{1}{\cancel{3}}}{\cancel{3} \times 5} = \frac{2}{5}$$

$$\frac{2}{3} \times \frac{3}{5} = \frac{2}{5}$$

Since you simplified before you multiplied, the answer should be in simplest terms.

You may be able to cancel more than once.

Example   Find $\frac{3}{4} \times \frac{2}{6}$.

- Look for the same factor in the numerator and the denominator.
- Divide. Cross out the original numbers and record the quotients.
- Look to see if there is another factor you can divide by. If there is, divide and record the quotients.
- Multiply. Use the numbers that result from canceling to multiply.

$$\frac{3}{4} \times \frac{2}{6} = \frac{\overset{1}{\cancel{3}} \times 2}{4 \times \underset{2}{\cancel{6}}}$$

$$= \frac{\overset{1}{\cancel{3}} \times \overset{1}{\cancel{2}}}{\underset{2}{\cancel{4}} \times \underset{2}{\cancel{6}}} = \frac{1}{4}$$

$$\frac{3}{4} \times \frac{2}{6} = \frac{1}{4}$$

The answer should be in simplest form. Check to see that it is.

PRACTICE

Write a number that is a factor of the numerator and also of the denominator.

Find each product. Cancel before you multiply. Be sure to check your answer to see if it is in simplest terms.

1. $\frac{3}{7} \times \frac{5}{9}$ _____

2. $\frac{4}{5} \times \frac{15}{17}$ _____

3. $\frac{6}{10} \times \frac{7}{12}$ _____

4. $\frac{1}{3} \times \frac{2}{5}$ _____

5. $\frac{3}{7} \times 21 =$

6. $\frac{2}{5} \times \frac{3}{8} =$

7. $5 \times \frac{4}{15} =$

8. $\frac{1}{4} \times \frac{2}{3} =$

9. $\frac{9}{10} \times \frac{2}{3} =$

10. $\frac{3}{8} \times \frac{2}{3} \times \frac{1}{5} =$

11. $\frac{4}{9} \times \frac{3}{7} \times \frac{1}{2} =$

12. $\frac{5}{6} \times \frac{2}{5} \times \frac{3}{7} =$

Rounding Fractions and Mixed Numbers

The rules for rounding fractions are similar to those for rounding decimal numbers.

- If a fraction is equal to or greater than $\frac{1}{2}$, round to the next greater whole number.
- If a fraction is less than $\frac{1}{2}$, the whole number remains the same.
- In either case, the fraction is dropped.

Examples

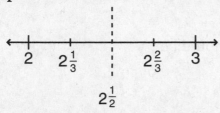

$\frac{5}{10}$ is between 0 and 1.

$\frac{5}{10} = \frac{1}{2}$

$\frac{5}{10}$ rounds to 1.

$2\frac{1}{3}$ is less than $2\frac{1}{2}$. $2\frac{2}{3}$ is greater than $2\frac{1}{2}$.

$2\frac{1}{3}$ rounds to 2. $2\frac{2}{3}$ rounds to 3.

To determine whether a fraction is less than, equal to, or greater than $\frac{1}{2}$, compare the numerator with the denominator.

- If the numerator is equal to half of the denominator, the fraction is equal to $\frac{1}{2}$.

Example $\frac{9}{18}$ 9 is half of 18, so $\frac{9}{18} = \frac{1}{2}$.

- If the numerator is less than half of the denominator, the fraction is less than $\frac{1}{2}$.

Example $\frac{4}{9}$ Half of 9 is $4\frac{1}{2}$, and 4 is less than $4\frac{1}{2}$, so $\frac{4}{9}$ is less than $\frac{1}{2}$.

- If the numerator is greater than half of the denominator, the fraction is greater than $\frac{1}{2}$.

Example $\frac{7}{12}$ Half of 12 is 6. 7 is greater than 6, so $\frac{7}{12}$ is greater than $\frac{1}{2}$.

PRACTICE

Round each amount to the nearest whole number.

1. $3\frac{1}{4} \approx$

2. $6\frac{1}{3} \approx$

3. $\frac{3}{4} \approx$

4. $9\frac{1}{10} \approx$

5. $25\frac{3}{5} \approx$

6. $2\frac{1}{4} \approx$

Round each amount to the nearest whole number. Then estimate the answer.

7. $1\frac{3}{4} + 1\frac{1}{2} \approx$

8. $4\frac{1}{2} \times 2\frac{1}{2} \approx$

9. $10\frac{1}{6} - 4\frac{6}{7} \approx$

Writing Fractions as Decimals

A fraction with 10, 100, 1,000, and so on, in its denominator is easily changed to a decimal.

Examples

Write $\frac{3}{10}$ as a decimal. $\frac{3}{10}$ = 3 tenths = 0.3

Write $\frac{51}{100}$ as a decimal. $\frac{51}{100}$ = 51 hundredths = 0.51

To rename other fractions to decimals, divide the numerator by the denominator.

Example   Name $\frac{1}{5}$ as a decimal.

- Write $\frac{1}{5}$ as a division problem.
- Write a decimal point after the 1 and place a decimal point above it in the quotient. Write a zero in the dividend after the decimal point.
- Divide. Place a zero in the ones place of the quotient.

$$5\overline{)1.0} \qquad \begin{array}{r} 0.2 \\ 5\overline{)1.0} \\ -1\ 0 \\ \hline 0 \end{array}$$

$$\frac{1}{5} = 0.2$$

Sometimes the division can be completed by adding one zero, as in the example above. Sometimes you need to add several zeros, as in the example at the left below. Sometimes, however, no matter how many zeros you add, the division either does not end, or the quotient has one or more digits that keep repeating, as in the example below at the right.)

Examples   Name $\frac{1}{8}$ as a decimal.

$$\begin{array}{r} 0.125 \\ 8\overline{)1.000} \\ -8 \\ \hline 20 \\ 16 \\ \hline 40 \\ -40 \\ \hline 0 \end{array}$$

$$\frac{1}{8} = 0.125$$

Name $\frac{1}{3}$ as a decimal.

$$\begin{array}{r} 0.333 \\ 3\overline{)1.000} \\ -9 \\ \hline 10 \\ -9 \\ \hline 10 \\ -9 \\ \hline 1 \end{array}$$

$$\frac{1}{3} = 0.333...*$$

* *Note:* The three dots show that the number keeps repeating. You can also write the number(s) that repeat with a bar over them. $0.333... = 0.\overline{3}$

PRACTICE

Write the decimal name for each fraction.

1. $\frac{3}{5}$ = _____

2. $\frac{1}{6}$ = _____

3. $\frac{1}{20}$ = _____

4. $\frac{1}{10}$ = _____

5. $\frac{2}{9}$ = _____

6. $\frac{2}{3}$ = _____

7. $\frac{4}{9}$ = _____

8. $\frac{7}{1,000}$ = _____

9. $\frac{3}{4}$ = _____

10. $\frac{17}{100}$ = _____

11. $\frac{1}{2}$ = _____

12. $\frac{9}{10}$ = _____

Writing Decimals as Fractions

A decimal can be written as a fraction that has a denominator of 10 or 100 or 1,000 and so on. Often, those fractions can be simplified to lower terms by dividing both the numerator and denominator by the same factor.

Example

Write 0.16 as a fraction.

- *Think*: 0.16 is 16 hundredths.
- Write 100 as the denominator of the fraction. $\frac{16}{100}$
- Write 16 as the numerator of the fraction.
- Simplify. $\frac{16 \div 4}{100 \div 4} = \frac{4}{25}$

$$0.16 = \frac{4}{25}$$ $\frac{16}{100} = \frac{4}{25}$

Example

Write 17.5 as a mixed number.

- *Think*: 17.5 is 17 and 5 tenths.
- Write the 5 tenths as a fraction $\frac{5}{10}$. $17.5 = 17\frac{5}{10}$
- Simplify the fraction $\frac{5}{10}$.
- Write 17.5 as a mixed number with $\frac{5}{10} = \frac{5 \div 5}{10 \div 5} = \frac{1}{2}$
  the reduced fraction of $\frac{1}{2}$.

$$17.5 = 17\frac{1}{2}$$ $17\frac{5}{10} = 17\frac{1}{2}$

PRACTICE

Write each decimal number as a fraction or mixed number in simplest terms.

1. 0.8 =

5. 0.9 =

9. 3.06 =

2. 0.70 =

6. 0.15 =

10. 0.21 =

3. 0.75 =

7. 1.8 =

11. 7.3 =

4. 2.4 =

8. 5.2 =

12. 0.6 =

Using Fractions to Solve Word Problems

Solve each word problem below. Reduce all your answers to simplest terms.

1. You are building a chair. The plans call for $\frac{1}{2}$-inch nails. Your nails are $\frac{3}{4}$ inch long. Are your nails too long or too short?

_____

2. There are 16 ounces in a pound. What fraction of a pound is 8 ounces?

_____

3. Mari needs 2 yards of scrap cloth. She finds five $\frac{1}{2}$-yard pieces. Does she have enough cloth?

_____

4. Your recipe calls for 300 grams of chocolate. You have 200 grams. What fraction of the chocolate do you have?

_____

5. Of the 125 people in the community choir, 22 of them actually come from other communities. What fraction of the choir comes from other communities?

_____

6. Two tablespoons of peanut butter have almost 0.25 of the Graciella's total carbohydrate allowance for a day. What fraction of her carbohydrate allowance is that?

_____

7. Martina ordered carpet that is $\frac{7}{8}$ of an inch thick. She ordered padding that is $\frac{5}{8}$ of an inch thick. When they are put together, how thick will they be?

_____

8. Yesterday it rained $\frac{3}{4}$ of an inch. Today it rained $\frac{1}{4}$ of an inch. How much rain has there been altogether?

_____

9. Ruby is growing tomato plants in her garden. Last week one plant was $2\frac{3}{4}$ feet tall. This week it is 3 feet tall. How much has it grown?

_____

10. Melinda is going to buy a crystal figure from a catalog. Her catalog says that the crystal cat is $1\frac{3}{8}$ inches tall. It says that the crystal baby is $1\frac{3}{4}$ inches tall. Which figure is taller?

_____

11. Your cookie recipe calls for $\frac{2}{3}$ cup of white sugar and $\frac{1}{3}$ cup of honey. How much sweetener do you need in all?

_____

12. John is doubling a cake recipe. The recipe calls for $\frac{1}{4}$ cup of butter. How much butter should John use?

_____

Writing Ratios

A **ratio** is a comparison of two quantities. A ratio can be written in three ways:

- using the word *to* 1 to 3
- with a colon 1 : 3
- as a fraction $\frac{1}{3}$

Statement	Things Being Compared	Ratio		
There are 4 men for every woman in the group.	men to women	4 to 1	4 : 1	$\frac{4}{1}$
He scores 1 free throw for every 3 he attempts.	free throws scored to attempts made	1 to 3	1 : 3	$\frac{1}{3}$
She drove 60 miles per hour.	miles to hours	60 to 1	60 : 1	$\frac{60}{1}$
One pound of chocolate costs $8.	pounds to dollars	1 to 8	1 : 8	$\frac{1}{8}$

Order is important. Notice that the order of the numbers in the ratios follows the order of the words in the comparison. In fraction form, the number mentioned first is the numerator and the second number is the denominator.

PRACTICE

Write the words for each comparison in fraction form. Then write the ratio as a fraction. The first one has been done for you. Remember, order is important.

1. Use 1 cup of ginger ale for every 3 cups of fruit juice.

   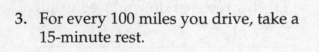

   $$\frac{\text{cups of ginger ale}}{\text{cups of juice}} \quad \frac{1}{3}$$

2. There are 2 teachers for every 31 students.

   _____

3. For every 100 miles you drive, take a 15-minute rest.

   _____

4. There are 4 quarts in 1 gallon.

   _____

5. On the highway, Janet's car gets 22 miles per gallon.

   _____

6. Admission is $12 per family.

   _____

7. It takes 20 minutes to pack each box.

   _____

8. Pablo earns $10 for each hour he works.

   _____

Recognizing a Proportion

Two ratios that are equal form a **proportion**.

Examples

If it costs $3 for 6 cans of soda, it costs $6 for 12 cans.

$$\frac{\$}{\text{cans}} \qquad \frac{3}{6} = \frac{6}{12}$$

If Joe runs 10 meters in 3 seconds, he will run
30 meters in 9 seconds.

$$\frac{\text{meters}}{\text{seconds}} \qquad \frac{10}{3} = \frac{30}{9}$$

When two ratios form a proportion, their **cross products** are equal.

Examples

$$\frac{3}{6} \overset{?}{\underset{\times}{=}} \frac{6}{12}$$

$$3 \times 12 \overset{?}{=} 6 \times 6$$

$$36 = 36$$

$\frac{3}{6}$ and $\frac{6}{12}$ form a proportion.

$$\frac{4}{5} \overset{?}{\underset{\times}{=}} \frac{12}{20}$$

$$4 \times 20 \overset{?}{=} 12 \times 5$$

$$80 \neq 60$$

$\frac{4}{5}$ and $\frac{12}{20}$ do not form a proportion.

PRACTICE

Use cross products to find out if the pair of ratios forms a proportion. For Numbers 5–12
you can rewrite the ratios in fraction form. Write = (equals) between each pair of ratios
that forms a proportion. Write ≠ (not equal) if the ratios are not a proportion.

1. $\frac{16}{2}$ $\frac{32}{4}$

2. $\frac{60}{1}$ $\frac{90}{2}$

3. $\frac{2}{3}$ $\frac{10}{15}$

4. $\frac{1}{4}$ $\frac{2}{9}$

5. 8 to 3   24 to 9

6. 7 to 4   35 to 28

7. 6 to 10   18 to 30

8. 15 to 32   8 to 20

9. 5 : 5   8 : 8

10. 1 : 4   7 : 21

11. 3 : 8   5 : 12

12. 16 : 7   15 : 6

Writing a Proportion

In a proportion, it is important to have numbers in the correct place. The numerators of the ratios must represent the same thing. The numbers in the denominators also must represent the same thing.

Example

Talia earns 3 award points for every 7 sales she makes.
Last week Talia made 49 sales, so she earned 21 award points.

In the above example, the comparison is points to sales.

- Write the words of the comparison in fraction form. Write the first ratio with the number for points in the numerator.

$$\frac{\text{points}}{\text{sales}} \qquad \frac{3}{7}$$

- Write the second ratio. Make sure the number for points is in the numerator.

$$\frac{\text{points}}{\text{sales}} \qquad \frac{3}{7} \quad \frac{21}{49}$$

- Check that the cross products are equal.

$$\frac{\text{points}}{\text{sales}} \qquad \frac{3}{7} \diagup\!\!\!\diagdown \frac{21}{49}$$

$$3 \times 49 \overset{?}{=} 21 \times 7$$
$$147 = 147$$

PRACTICE

Use the two ratios to write a proportion for each situation. Check that the cross products are equal.

1. Ryan packs 4 boxes each hour. In 8 hours he packs 32 boxes.

   _____

2. It takes 64 sheets of paper to make 1 book. It will take 448 sheets of paper to make 7 books.

   _____

3. Ramona plants 1 red flower for every 3 yellow flowers. Yesterday she planted 24 yellow flowers and 8 red ones.

   _____

4. Jason's car gets 15 miles to a gallon. If Jason drives 75 miles, he will use 5 gallons of gas.

   _____

Circle _Y_ if the description is a proportion. Circle _N_ if it is not.

5. The factory produces 25 cars every 2 hours. In 8 hours, it produces 100 cars. Y N

6. Yvonne types 60 words a minute. In 3 minutes, she types 180 words. Y N

7. When yogurt was on sale at 10 containers for $5, Jean bought 2 containers for $1. Y N

8. If an airplane is traveling at 500 miles per hour, in 4 hours it will travel 2,000 miles. Y N

Solving a Proportion

Proportions are often used to solve problems. If you know three of the numbers of a proportion, you can use cross products to find the fourth.

Example

At Flo's Floral Shop, 12 roses cost $27.
How much will 36 roses cost?

- Write a proportion. Be careful to write each number in the correct position. Write a letter in the place of the missing number.

$$\frac{\text{roses}}{\text{dollars}} \qquad \frac{12}{27} = \frac{36}{n}$$

- Find cross products.

$$12 \times n = 27 \times 36$$
$$12\,n = 972$$

- Divide on both sides of the equal sign. Divide by the number multiplying n.

$$12\,n \div 12 = 972 \div 12$$
$$n = 81$$

It will cost $81 for 36 roses.

PRACTICE

Find the missing number to complete each proportion. Use cross products to check your answers.

1. $\dfrac{5}{12} = \dfrac{20}{\square}$

   $\square = \underline{\hspace{2cm}}$

2. $\dfrac{2}{5} = \dfrac{\square}{20}$

   $\square = \underline{\hspace{2cm}}$

3. $\dfrac{8}{10} = \dfrac{\square}{30}$

   $\square = \underline{\hspace{2cm}}$

4. $\dfrac{7}{13} = \dfrac{21}{\square}$

   $\square = \underline{\hspace{2cm}}$

5. $\dfrac{6}{15} = \dfrac{\square}{45}$

   $\square = \underline{\hspace{2cm}}$

6. $\dfrac{12}{20} = \dfrac{\square}{60}$

   $\square = \underline{\hspace{2cm}}$

7. $\dfrac{9}{14} = \dfrac{18}{\square}$

   $\square = \underline{\hspace{2cm}}$

8. $\dfrac{4}{9} = \dfrac{\square}{36}$

   $\square = \underline{\hspace{2cm}}$

Write a proportion and solve for the missing number.

9. Samuel drives 50 miles in 1 hour. How many miles will he drive in 3 hours?

   _____

10. Abby saves $15 each month. How many months will it take her to save $150?

    _____

11. It takes Ted 2 days to paint 3 rooms. How many days will it take him to paint 15 rooms?

    _____

12. For every pound of dark chocolate sold, the candy shop sells about 3 pounds of milk chocolate. If they sell 18 pounds of milk chocolate, about how many pounds of dark chocolate will be sold?

    _____

Fractions Skills Checkup

Circle the letter of the correct answer to each problem. Simplify all fractions to lowest terms.

1.

$$\frac{5}{7} + \frac{3}{7} =$$

A $\frac{2}{7}$ C $\frac{4}{7}$

B 8   D $1\frac{1}{7}$

E None of these

2.

$$\frac{5}{12} - \frac{1}{12} =$$

F $\frac{1}{4}$ H $\frac{1}{6}$

G $\frac{1}{12}$ J $\frac{1}{3}$

K None of these

3.

$$7 \times \frac{4}{7} =$$

A 7   C 4

B $1\frac{3}{4}$ D $1\frac{4}{7}$

E None of these

4.

$$\frac{3}{4} \times \frac{2}{5} =$$

F $\frac{5}{9}$ H $\frac{2}{3}$

G $\frac{1}{4}$ J $\frac{2}{5}$

K None of these

5.

$$\frac{25}{5} =$$

A 5   C $\frac{1}{5}$

B 10   D 25

E None of these

6.

$$\frac{3}{5}$$

$$+ \frac{4}{5}$$

F $\frac{7}{10}$ H $2\frac{2}{5}$

G $1\frac{2}{5}$ J $\frac{12}{25}$

K None of these

7. The Cougars won 4 games and lost 8. Which of these does *not* show the ratio of games won to games lost?

A 4 to 8   C 8 : 4

B $\frac{4}{8}$ D 4 : 8

8. You can buy 3 pounds of sliced cheese for $5. How many pounds can you buy for $25?

F 9 pounds   H 12 pounds
G 15 pounds   J 18 pounds

9. Which number is a factor of 9 and also a factor of 15?

A 9   C 5
B 4   D 3

10. Which of these is equal to $\frac{16}{20}$ in simplest terms?

F $\frac{3}{4}$ H $\frac{2}{3}$

G $\frac{7}{8}$ J $\frac{4}{5}$

11. What is another name for 0.25?

A $\frac{1}{4}$ C $\frac{1}{2}$

B $\frac{1}{5}$ D $\frac{1}{3}$

12. What is another name for $\frac{3}{5}$?

F 0.3   H 0.8
G 0.6   J 0.9

13.

$\dfrac{6}{7} - \dfrac{2}{7} =$

- A $\dfrac{4}{14}$
- B $\dfrac{3}{7}$
- C 4
- D $\dfrac{4}{7}$
- E None of these

14.

$\dfrac{1}{2} \times \dfrac{1}{5} \times \dfrac{1}{8} =$

- F $\dfrac{1}{15}$
- G $\dfrac{3}{15}$
- H $\dfrac{1}{80}$
- J $\dfrac{3}{80}$
- K None of these

15.

$\dfrac{1}{6} \times \dfrac{7}{5} =$

- A $\dfrac{8}{30}$
- B $\dfrac{7}{11}$
- C $\dfrac{7}{30}$
- D $\dfrac{8}{11}$
- E None of these

16. $\dfrac{4}{5} - \dfrac{4}{6} =$

- F $\dfrac{1}{2}$
- G $\dfrac{1}{4}$
- H $\dfrac{1}{3}$
- J 3
- K None of these

17.

$\dfrac{7}{10} - \dfrac{7}{10} =$

- A 1
- B 7
- C 0
- D $\dfrac{1}{10}$
- E None of these

18.

$\dfrac{12}{12} =$

- F 12
- G 0
- H 2
- J 1
- K None of these

19. Which number sentence is true?

- A $\dfrac{1}{2} < \dfrac{1}{3}$
- B $\dfrac{6}{5} < 1$
- C $\dfrac{11}{12} < 1$
- D $\dfrac{4}{5} < \dfrac{1}{2}$

20. Which set of fractions is in order from least to greatest?

- F $\dfrac{1}{12}, \dfrac{1}{2}, \dfrac{1}{3}$
- G $\dfrac{1}{2}, \dfrac{1}{3}, \dfrac{1}{12}$
- H $\dfrac{1}{2}, \dfrac{1}{12}, \dfrac{1}{3}$
- J $\dfrac{1}{12}, \dfrac{1}{3}, \dfrac{1}{2}$

21. Ginger ran $\dfrac{7}{3}$ miles. Which of these is equal to $\dfrac{7}{3}$ miles?

- A $1\dfrac{2}{3}$ miles
- B 2 miles
- C $2\dfrac{1}{3}$ miles
- D 3 miles

22. Which is the best estimate for the sum of $2\dfrac{7}{8} + 2\dfrac{4}{5}$?

- F 4
- G 5
- H $4\dfrac{3}{2}$
- J 6

23. Ella types about 60 words per minute. At that rate, about how long should it take her to type a paragraph that contains 840 words?

- A 14 minutes
- B 25 minutes
- C 20 minutes
- D 30 minutes

Decimals

Identifying Decimal Place Value

Decimal fractions are numbers that are less than 1.
A **decimal point** is used to separate decimal fractions,
more simply called **decimals**, from whole numbers.

Our place-value system can help us read and write
decimals. The first three decimal columns to the right of the
decimal point are tenths, hundredths, and thousandths.
Notice that each decimal place value ends with *–ths*. Notice,
too, that the place-value names on either side of the ones column are similar; tens on the left
of the ones and tenths on the right, hundreds on the left and hundredths on the right,
thousands on the left and thousandths on the right, and so on.

PRACTICE

Write the digit in the place named.

In the tenths place

1. 28.67 _____

2. 0.9872 _____

3. 135.627 _____

4. 8.3 _____

In the hundredths place

5. 6.729 _____

6. 15.904 _____

7. 2.96 _____

8. 14.0578 _____

In the thousandths place

9. 5.057 _____

10. 0.3728 _____

11. 120.126 _____

12. 0.7531 _____

Write the place value of the 8 in each number.

13. 3.872 _____

14. 26.0381 _____

15. 0.1849 _____

16. 18.420 _____

Identify each place value.

17. The third digit to the right of (after) the decimal point

_____

18. The first digit to the right of (after) the decimal point

_____

19. The first digit to the left of (before) the decimal point

_____

20. The second digit to the right of (after) the decimal point

_____

Reading and Writing Decimals

To read a decimal, start at the decimal point and read the number as if you were reading a whole number. Then say the place-value name of the digit farthest to the right.

Examples

0.9 nine tenths   0.18 eighteen hundredths
0.30 thirty hundredths   0.235 two hundred thirty-five thousandths

When there is a whole number together with a decimal, read the whole number, say *and* for the decimal point, then read the decimal. Be sure not to say *and* anywhere but for the decimal point when you say the number.

Examples

26.7 twenty-six and seven tenths   6.09 six and nine hundredths

PRACTICE

Match the number to the words. Write the letter of the number on the line in front of the words.

A 0.140   B 1.04   C 0.7   D 0.07   E 0.014   F 0.70

_____ 1. seven hundredths   _____ 4. seven tenths

_____ 2. one and four hundredths   _____ 5. fourteen thousandths

_____ 3. seventy hundredths   _____ 6. one hundred forty thousandths

To write a decimal from words, think about the number of digits needed to the right of the decimal point. Remember, the word *and* means decimal point.

Examples

three tenths	tenths—1 digit to the right of the decimal point	0.3
three hundredths	hundredths—2 digits to the right of the decimal point	0.03
three thousandths	thousandths—3 digits to the right of the decimal point	0.003
ten and eight tenths	whole number and 1 decimal place	10.8
five and six hundredths	whole number and 2 decimal places	5.06

PRACTICE

Write each number in words. Remember to write *and* for the decimal point if there is a whole number together with a decimal.

7. 0.6 _____   10. 10.1 _____

8. 0.01 _____   11. 0.125 _____

9. 3.05 _____   12. 40.100 _____

Relating Decimals and Fractions

A decimal can be written as a fraction with a denominator of 10 or 100 or 1,000, and so on.

Decimal	Words	Fraction
0.3	three tenths	$\frac{3}{10}$
0.06	six hundredths	$\frac{6}{100}$
0.012	twelve thousandths	$\frac{12}{1,000}$

Example   Write 0.6 as a fraction.
- Use the decimal place you say after the number to determine the denominator of the fraction.
    If you say tenths, the denominator will be 10.
    If you say hundredths, the denominator will be 100, and so on.
    0.6 $\longrightarrow$ say six tenths $\longrightarrow$ write 10 in the denominator
- Write the number you say as the numerator.
    0.6 $\longrightarrow$ say six tenths $\longrightarrow$ write 6 in the numerator

$$0.6 = \frac{6}{10}$$

PRACTICE

Name the shaded part of each square as a decimal and as a fraction.

1. _____

2. _____

3. _____

4. _____

Write each number as a fraction and as a decimal.

5. twenty-four thousandths

_____

6. nineteen hundredths

_____

7. one hundred hundredths

_____

8. nine hundred nine thousandths

_____

9. one and six tenths

_____

10. three and three hundredths

_____

Recognizing Equivalent Decimals

Adding zeros after the digits at the right of the decimal point does *not* change the value of the amount named

Example

0.2 names part of a whole that is divided into 10 equal parts.

0.20 names the same amount of that whole when the whole is divided into 100 equal parts.

0.200 also names the same amount of the whole. Here, the whole is divided into 1,000 equal parts.

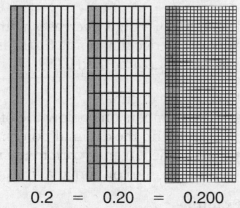

0.2 = 0.20 = 0.200

A decimal point and zeros can be added after the ones place of a whole number. This does not change the value, but it does change the way you read the number.

Examples

1 = 1.0	1 = 1 and 0 tenths	1 is also equal to 10 tenths.
1 = 1.00	1 = 1 and 0 hundredths	1 is also equal to 100 hundredths.
1 = 1.000	1 = 1 and 0 thousandths	1 is also equal to 1,000 thousandths.

PRACTICE

Equal amounts of the figures in each pair are shaded. Write the number to complete the name of the shaded portion. Then write each amount as a decimal.

1.

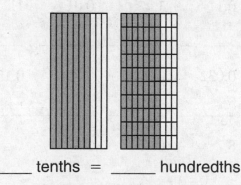

_____ tenths = _____ hundredths

_____ = _____

2.

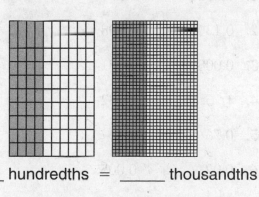

_____ hundredths = _____ thousandths

_____ = _____

Circle each pair of numbers that name an equal amount.

3.	0.75	0.7	6.	14.9	14.09	9.	5.07	5.070
4.	0.6	0.600	7.	2	2.0	10.	0.4	0.040
5.	2.05	2.050	8.	0.30	0.300	11.	8	8.00

Comparing Decimal Numbers

Unlike whole numbers, with decimals, a greater number of digits does not necessarily mean a greater amount.

The value of a digit decreases with each place to the right of the decimal point. So 0.4 is greater than 0.04, and 0.04 is greater than 0.004.

To compare decimals
• Write numbers one below the other. Line up digits by lining up the decimal points.
• Start at the left and work to the right. Compare one column at a time.

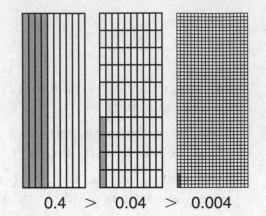

0.4 > 0.04 > 0.004

Examples

Compare 0.5 and 0.289.

```
0 . 5
0 . 2 8 9
```

5 tenths is greater than 2 tenths.

0.5 > 0.289

Compare 0.882 and 0.89.

```
0 . 8 8 2
0 . 8 9
```

8 hundredths is less than 9 hundredths.

0.882 < 0.89

PRACTICE

Circle the lesser number in each pair.

1. 0.003   0.87

2. 0.13   0.098

3. 0.00899   0.051

4. 1.75   1.032

5. 0.76   0.13

6. 0.02   0.005

Circle the least number in each row.

7. 0.51   0.09   1.3

8. 11   0.19   1.023

9. 1.6   1.8   1.05

10. 0.13   0.07   0.002

Arrange each set of numbers from least to greatest.

11. 0.1   1   0.01   11

_____ , _____ , _____ , _____

12. 0.032   0.023   0.75   0.15

_____ , _____ , _____ , _____

13. 8.7   0.75   2.3

_____ , _____ , _____

14. 3.07   30.7   0.37   0.73

_____ , _____ , _____ , _____

Rearrange the digits to make the _greatest_ decimal possible.

15. 3 9 5 1   0. _____

16. 7 8 1 3   0. _____

Adding Decimals

To add decimals, write the numbers below one another in columns. Line up digits to add tenths to tenths, hundredths to hundredths, and so on. Lining up the decimal points will help. Then add as usual, regrouping as needed. Be sure to place a decimal point in the answer.

Examples

Add 4.3 + 0.93.

- Write numbers below one another, lining up decimal points.
- Fill each column by writing 0 if there is no digit.
- Add.
- Write a decimal point in the answer. Decimal points should line up vertically.

$$
\begin{array}{r} 4.3 \\ + 0.93 \end{array} \rightarrow
\begin{array}{r} \text{Start} \\ \downarrow \\ \overset{1}{4.30} \\ + 0.93 \\ \hline 5.23 \end{array}
$$

4.3 + 0.93 = 5.23

Add 6 + 2.5 + 0.14.

- Write a decimal point to the right of the ones place of a whole number.
- Write numbers below one another, lining up decimal points.
- Fill each column by writing 0 if there is no digit.
- Add.
- Write a decimal point in the answer. Decimal points should line up vertically.

$$
\begin{array}{r} 6.00 \\ 2.50 \\ + 0.14 \\ \hline 8.64 \end{array}
$$

6 + 2.5 + 0.14 = 8.64

PRACTICE

Find each sum.

1.
$$
\begin{array}{r} 5.6 \\ + \ 3. \end{array}
\qquad
\begin{array}{r} 0.14 \\ + \ 0.32 \end{array}
\qquad
\begin{array}{r} \$1.00 \\ + \ \$1.60 \end{array}
\qquad
\begin{array}{r} 1.09 \\ + \ 0.05 \end{array}
\qquad
\begin{array}{r} 2. \\ + \ 0.62 \end{array}
\qquad
\begin{array}{r} 1. \\ + \ 0.03 \end{array}
$$

Rewrite problems in column form, then add.

2. 0.19 + 3 = _____

3. 0.075 + 0.123 = _____

4. 0.238 + 6 = _____

5. 0.12 + 0.07 = _____

6. 6 + 0.012 = _____

7. 52.8 + 0.15 = _____

8. 5 + 0.264 = _____

9. 0.52 + 1.3 = _____

10. 23.02 + 0.095 = _____

Subtracting Decimals

To subtract decimals, write the number being subtracted below the starting amount. Line up the decimal points to line up the digits. As with adding decimals, write zeros to fill spaces where there are no digits. Then subtract as usual, regrouping as needed. Be sure to place a decimal point in the answer.

Example

Find 12.7 − 0.66.

- Write numbers below one another, lining up decimal points.
- Fill each column by writing 0 if there is no digit.
- Subtract.
- Write a decimal point in the answer.
  Decimal points should line up vertically.

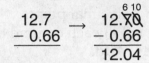

12.7 − 0.66 = 12.04

PRACTICE

Find each difference.

1.	7.9	0.74	$9.00	0.10	2.	7.56
	− 5.	− 0.71	− $1.75	− 0.05	− 0.62	− 0.08

Rewrite problems in column form, then subtract.

2. 0.25 − 0.15 = _____

3. 6.6 − 0.13 = _____

4. 0.2 − 0.078 = _____

5. 30 − 12.7 = _____

6. 0.8 − 0.06 = _____

7. 1.09 − 0.25 = _____

8. 0.903 − 0.16 = _____

9. 4 − 0.57 = _____

10. 0.09 − 0.03 = _____

11. 11.3 − 0.113 = _____

12. 6 − 2.556 = _____

13. 16.5 − 3.04 = _____

Multiplying Decimals

When you multiply decimals, do *not* line up the decimal points. Multiply as with whole numbers. Count the decimal places in each factor—the total of the decimal places is the number of decimal places that should be in the answer.

Example

Multiply 0.15 × 0.03.

$$\begin{array}{r} 0.15 \\ \times\ 0.03 \\ \hline 45 \end{array}$$

- Ignore decimal points and multiply as with whole numbers.

- Count the decimal places in each factor and find the total. There is a total of 4 decimal places.

$$\begin{array}{r} 0.15 \leftarrow 2 \text{ decimal places} \\ \times\ 0.03 \leftarrow 2 \text{ decimal places} \\ \hline 45 \leftarrow 4 \text{ decimal places} \end{array}$$

- Write the decimal point in the product. Start at the right and count 4 places to the left. Write zeros to the left of the product to get additional places.

- Write a zero in the ones place.

$$\begin{array}{r} 0.15 \\ \times\ 0.03 \\ \hline 0.0045 \end{array}$$

0.15 × 0.03 = 0.0045

PRACTICE

Find each product. If there is a dollar sign in the problem, be sure to place the dollar sign in the answer.

1. $\begin{array}{r} 0.3 \\ \times\ 0.6 \\ \hline \end{array}$

2. $\begin{array}{r} 1.3 \\ \times\ 0.2 \\ \hline \end{array}$

3. $\begin{array}{r} \$5.40 \\ \times\ 5 \\ \hline \end{array}$

4. $\begin{array}{r} \$0.75 \\ \times\ 3 \\ \hline \end{array}$

5. $\begin{array}{r} 2.5 \\ \times\ 0.3 \\ \hline \end{array}$

6. $\begin{array}{r} 0.305 \\ \times\ 5 \\ \hline \end{array}$

7. $\begin{array}{r} \$3.33 \\ \times\ 15 \\ \hline \end{array}$

8. $\begin{array}{r} \$0.15 \\ \times\ 3 \\ \hline \end{array}$

9. $\begin{array}{r} 0.12 \\ \times\ 0.3 \\ \hline \end{array}$

10. $\begin{array}{r} 0.21 \\ \times\ 0.4 \\ \hline \end{array}$

11. $\begin{array}{r} 4.2 \\ \times\ 0.5 \\ \hline \end{array}$

12. $\begin{array}{r} 0.75 \\ \times\ 0.4 \\ \hline \end{array}$

13. $\begin{array}{r} 0.06 \\ \times\ 0.7 \\ \hline \end{array}$

14. $\begin{array}{r} 0.31 \\ \times\ 0.2 \\ \hline \end{array}$

15. $\begin{array}{r} 0.05 \\ \times\ 0.09 \\ \hline \end{array}$

Rounding Decimals

Rounding decimals is similar to rounding with whole numbers. But when you round a decimal, the number ends with the decimal place you round to.

To round to the nearest whole number, look at the digit in the tenths place.

- If the tenths digit is 5 or greater increase the whole number by 1. Delete digits to the right of the ones place.

- If the digit in the tenths place is 4 or less, just delete tenths digit and any digits to the right of it.

Examples

0.⑦ rounds to 1   0.③ rounds to 0

5.⑤2 rounds to 6   6.⓪4 rounds to 6

2.⑧01 rounds to 3   0.④9999 rounds to 0

Note: When rounded to the nearest whole number, the number will end with the ones digit.

To round to the nearest tenth, look at the hundredths digit.

- If the digit in the hundredths place is 5 or greater, increase the tenths digit by 1. Delete digits to the right of the tenths place.

- If the digit in the hundredths place is 4 or less, just delete the hundredths digit and any digits to the right.

Examples

5.6⑥8 rounds to 5.7   3.8④2 rounds to 3.8

18.0③ rounds to 18.0   0.0③ rounds to 0.0

0.9④3 rounds to 0.9   9.9⑥ rounds to 10.0

Note: When rounded to the nearest tenth, the number will end with the tenths digit.

PRACTICE

Round to the nearest whole number.

1. 0.62 _____

2. 12.098 _____

3. 24.7 _____

4. 4.03 _____

5. 6.97 _____

6. 180.227 _____

7. 8.710 _____

8. 2.503 _____

9. 300.57 _____

10. Carmine has $24.85. About how much money does Carmine have? _____

Round to the nearest tenth.

11. 0.823 _____

12. 7.15 _____

13. 0.05 _____

14. 0.04 _____

15. 0.15 _____

16. 9.77 _____

17. 32.006 _____

18. 0.95 _____

19. 9.905

20. To win the contest, Sunny needs at least 15.5 points. Scores are totaled and then rounded to the nearest tenth. Sunny has 15.295 points. Will she win? _____

Using Decimals to Solve Word Problems

Review the five steps for solving word problems. Use these steps to solve the problems below.

- **Identify the question**. Try to put the question in your own words.
- **Determine what information you need**. Is the information given, or do you need additional information?
- **Make a plan**. Decide whether to add, subtract, multiply, or divide. Look for clue words that will help you.
- **Solve the problem**. Follow your plan.
- **Check your work**. Did you answer the question? Does your answer make sense? Is it reasonable? Is your computation correct?

PRACTICE

Circle the letter for the number sentence that shows how to solve each problem.

1. Mia ordered 2 jackets through the mail. One weighed 1.3 kilograms (kg). The other weighed 3.15 kilograms. What was the total weight of the order?

   A $3.15 \text{ kg} - 1.3 \text{ kg} = \boxed{} \text{ kg}$

   B $3.15 \text{ kg} \times 1.3 \text{ kg} = \boxed{} \text{ kg}$

   C $3.15 \text{ kg} + 1.3 \text{ kg} = \boxed{} \text{ kg}$

   D Not enough information given

2. Experts predict that girls born in 2000 will live an average of 79.7 years. They predict boys born that year will live an average of 74.3 years. How much longer are the women expected to live than the men?

   F $79.7 + 74.3 = \boxed{} \text{ years}$

   G $74.3 - 79.7 = \boxed{} \text{ years}$

   H $79.7 - 74.3 = \boxed{} \text{ years}$

   J Not enough information given

Find the answer for each problem. Be sure to include the unit of measure in your answer.

3. Omar has 12 boards. Each is 2.3 feet long. How many feet of board does he have in all?

   _____

4. One box of cereal weighs 0.75 pounds. How much do 50 boxes of cereal weigh?

   _____

5. Marge measured around the edge of a blanket to see how much trim she would need. As she measured each side, she wrote down the measurements: 65.75 inches, 40.23 inches, 65.75 inches, and 40.23 inches. How many inches of trim does she need in all?

   _____

6. Coco drove to New York. When she began the trip, her mileage odometer was at 11,545.6 miles. When she got to New York, it read 11,966.9 miles. How many miles did she drive?

   _____

Decimals Skills Checkup

Circle the letter for the correct answer to each problem. Try crossing out unreasonable answers before you start to work on each problem.

1. $15 + 3.1 =$
   A 153.1
   B 15.31
   C 1.81
   D 4.6
   E None of these

2. $5.1 - 0.06 =$
   F 5.4
   G 4.4
   H 5.04
   J 4.04
   K None of these

3. $0.04 \times 4 =$
   A 16
   B 1.6
   C 0.16
   D 4.04
   E None of these

4. $\$8.22 \times 3 =$
   F $24.22
   G $24.55
   H $24.66
   J $11.66
   K None of these

5. $2.3 + 6.4 =$
   A 8.43
   B 8.34
   C 8.7
   D 23.64
   E None of these

6. $\begin{array}{r} 45.2 \\ -3.9 \\ \end{array}$
   F 0.413
   G 49.1
   H 42.3
   J 41.3
   K None of these

7. Julio earns an average of $31.50 a night in tips. At this rate, about how much will he earn in 5 nights?
   A $ 50
   B $ 75
   C $150
   D $175

8. Jerry earns $14.80 per hour. Yesterday he worked for 5.25 hours. Which number sentence should he use to estimate how much he earned yesterday?
   F $\$14 \times 5 = \square$
   G $\$15 \times 5 = \square$
   H $\$14 \times 6 = \square$
   J $\$15 \times 6 = \square$

9. Link's cleaning bill came to $18.46. He paid with a $20 bill. How much change should he receive?
   A $1.44
   B $2.44
   C $1.54
   D $2.54

10. Obami is buying shades for her windows. They cost $6 each, and she has 7 windows. How much will she spend?
    F $76
    G $49
    H $42
    J $13

11.

$0.3 + 0.7 =$

A 1
B 0.1
C 1.1
D 0.9
E None of these

12.

$$\begin{array}{r} 0.3 \\ \times \quad 6 \\ \hline \end{array}$$

F 0.18
G 18
H 1.8
J 1.08
K None of these

13.

$$\begin{array}{r} 1 \\ - \quad 0.2 \\ \hline \end{array}$$

A 8
B 0.8
C 0.08
D 80
E None of these

14.

$$\begin{array}{r} 98.0 \\ - \quad 5.15 \\ \hline \end{array}$$

F 46.5
G 93.95
H 92.85
J 93.85
K None of these

15.

$1.402 \times 0.2 =$

A 0.284
B 28.04
C 0.2804
D 2.804
E None of these

16.

$$\begin{array}{r} 5.1 \\ \times \quad 2.3 \\ \hline \end{array}$$

F 11.73
G 2.55
H 25.5
J 117.3
K None of these

17.

$25 + 3.5 =$

A 60
B 6
C 0.6
D 28.5
E None of these

18. Which set of decimal numbers is in order from least to greatest?

F 1, 1.07, 0.8, 0.09
G 0.8, 1, 0.09, 1.07
H 0.8, 0.09, 1, 1.07
J 0.09, 0.8, 1, 1.07

19. A number begins with the digit 0 and a decimal point. Then it uses the digits 1, 6, 5, and 0, each exactly once. What is the smallest decimal that can be written?

A 0.0651
B 0.6510
C 0.1560
D 0.0156

20. What is 19.079 rounded to the nearest tenth?

F 20
G 19
H 19.1
J 19.08

21. An average of 3.13 inches of rain fell in June. An average of 3.5 inches fell in July. How much greater was the average rainfall in July than in June?

A 0.37 inches
B 8.63 inches
C 10.96 inches
D 3.13 inches

22. Frank bought 185 pens to give as gifts to his customers. The pens cost $3.87 each. Which is the best estimate of the cost of the pens?

F $200   H $600
G $400   J $800

Data Analysis

Reading a Table

Tables and graphs are used to organize and display information so it can be read quickly. To understand a table, it is important to read the title and the headings. The **title** tells what the table is about. The **headings** tell what information is found in the columns. The information related to each row is found in the columns.

The **title** is the main description of the table.

Read each **column** from top to bottom.

Headings describe the columns.

Read each **row** from left to right.

Volunteers for the Fundraiser

Job	Number of Volunteers	Group Leader
Answering Phones	12	R. Miller
Making Deliveries	15	M. Lopez
Cleaning	6	T. Sanks
Cooking	8	F. Chu

PRACTICE

Use the table above to answer each question.

1. What does this table describe?

   A telephones
   B different types of jobs
   C cooking
   D people who are helping out at a fundraiser

2. What is this part of the table called?

Making Deliveries	15	M. Lopez

   F a column
   G a row
   H a heading
   J the title

3. What does this column in the table tell you?

12
15
6
8

   A the number of hours each person worked
   B the number of phones
   C the number of people who offered to help with each job
   D There is no way to tell.

4. What is found in the third column of the table?

   F the person who is leading each group of workers
   G cleaning
   H cooking
   J the names of the people who wrote the table

Exact information can be found in the box, or cell, where the row and column meet.

Video Bargain's Rental Fees

	Number of Days		
	1	3	5
Regular Videos	$1.00	$2.00	$3.00
New Releases	$2.50	$5.00	$7.50
Video Games	$1.75	$3.25	$6.50

Example

What does Video Bargain charge to rent a regular video for 5 days?
- Find the row labeled *Regular Videos*.
- Find the *Days* column for *5 days*.
- Go across the row and down the column to find where the two meet. That cell has the information you are looking for.

Video bargain charges $3 to rent a regular video for 5 days.

PRACTICE

Use the table above to answer these questions.

5. How much does it cost to rent a regular video for 3 days? _____

6. How much does it cost to rent a video game for 5 days? _____

7. You rent a video game for 3 days and a regular video for 3 days. How much do you pay? _____

8. What can you rent for $1.35 or less? _____

9. Which type of video is the most expensive to rent? _____

10. What is the fee for renting a new release for 3 days? _____

11. *Revenge of the Zombies* just came out on video, and this store has it. Which row tells the cost to rent this movie?

    _____

12. You rent 2 video games on Monday and return them on Friday. What is the fee?

    _____

13. Which of these can be found in the table?

    A the charge for losing a video
    B whether this store is more expensive than others
    C the cost to rent a video
    D whether this store sells snacks
    E whether this store has foreign films

Using Numbers in a Table

You can use the numbers in a table to find additional information.

Examples

How many more years than Heidi has David been
with the company?
> Subtract to find the difference.
> Heidi = 5 years; David = 10 years   10 − 5 = 5

Heidi has been with the company **5** more years.

Clinton has been with the company 5 times as long
as what other worker?
> Divide the number of years for Clinton by 5.
> Clinton = 10 years; 10 ÷ 5 = 2

Linda has been with the company **2** years.
Clinton has been with the company 5 times as long as Linda.

Years with the Company

Employee	Years of Service
Anne Rodriguez	25
Clinton Reed	10
Linda Hansen	2
David Blume	10
Heidi Hunt	5
Myumi Kino	8

PRACTICE

Use the table above to fill in the blanks.

1. Who has been with this company the shortest time? _____

2. Who has been with the company longer, Myumi or David? _____

3. How much longer has Clinton been with the company than Heidi? _____

4. Who has been with the company 20 years longer than Heidi? _____

5. Who has been with the company 4 times as long as Linda? _____

6. How much longer than Clinton has Anne been with the company? _____

Use the table below for Numbers 7–9.

School Scores on State Test

School	Reading	Writing	Math
Lincoln	70	64	35
Thorpe	73	69	42
Tubman	86	73	57
Wiley	72	63	32
Roosevelt	64	55	32

7. Which school had the highest math score? _____

8. Which school had the lowest writing score? _____

9. Lincoln's reading scores were how many times higher than their math scores? _____

Using a Price List

A price list is a commonly used type of table. Items are listed in a column with prices across from them—you find the item and look across for its price. If you need to find the total of several prices, it is a good idea to write each one and then do any figuring.

Swiftcopy Price List		
Copies		
Per Sheet	Single-sided	Double-sided
$8\frac{1}{2} \times 11$ B/W*	$0.08	$0.13
11×17 B/W	0.25	0.40
$8\frac{1}{2} \times 11$ Color	0.65	1.10
Add 2 cents per page for colored paper.		
Other Services		
Laminating	$2.50 per sheet	
Spiral binding	$1.50 per packet	
Plastic covers	$2.50 per book	

*B/W = Black and White

PRACTICE

Use the price list above to answer these questions. Figure $8\frac{1}{2}$ x 11 paper unless a problem calls for a different size.

1. How much would it cost to have 20 single-sided black and white copies on white paper? _____

2. How much more would it cost to have the 20 single-sided copies printed on colored paper? _____

3. If you have 1 double-sided copy printed on 11 x 17 paper and then have it laminated, how much will it cost? _____

4. You have 20 double-sided copies printed on white paper. You then have the copies put together with a spiral binding. What is the total cost? _____

5. How much will it cost for 10 single-sided color copies? _____

6. Laura needs 10 double-sided copies. How much more will it cost for color than for black and white? _____

7. How many black and white double-sided copies can Jason have made for 80 cents? _____

8. Clarence needs 50 single-sided black and white copies. How much can he save if he has the pages printed on two sides of the paper instead of just one? _____

Finding Mean, Median, and Mode

When talking about a set of data, it is often useful to have a typical number to represent the data. Three ways to find a typical number for the data are to calculate the **mean**, the **median**, and the **mode**. The data in the table "Years with the Company" is used in the examples below.

Years with the Company

Employee	Years of Service
Anne Rodriguez	25
Clinton Reed	10
Linda Hansen	2
David Blume	10
Heidi Hunt	5
Myumi Kino	8

Mean

Mean is another word for **average**. To find the mean, or average, add up all of the values and then divide the total by the number of values you added.

Example   What is the average number of years of service for the six people at the company?

- Add the number of years together. $25 + 10 + 2 + 10 + 5 + 8 = 60$
- Divide by 6, the number of people. $60 \div 6 = 10$

The average number of years of service is 10 years.

Median

The median is the number in the middle of the set of numbers that are arranged in order from least to greatest. Half of the numbers in the set will be greater than the median and half will be less than the median.

Example   What is the median number of years the workers have been with the company?

- Write the numbers in order from least to greatest.   2, 5, 8, 10, 10, 25
- Circle the number in center of the list. In this set of data there is an even number of values, so there are 2 center values.   2, 5, (8, 10,)10, 25
- When there are 2 center values, find their average. $10 + 8 = 18$ $18 \div 2 = 9$

The median number of years the workers have been with the company is 9 years.

Mode

The mode is the number that appears most often in a set of numbers. There can be more than one mode. If no number appears more often than others, there is no mode.

Example   What is the mode for the data in the chart of years with the company?

- Write the numbers in the set of data.   25, 10, 2, 10, 5, 8
- Look to see if one number appears more often than the others. In this set of data, the number 10 appears twice. All other numbers appear once.

The mode of the data is 10 years.

Complete the table.

1.

Bargains Galore Telephone Orders

Operator	Minutes Spent on Each Call						Median	Mode	Mean
	1	2	3	4	5	6			
A	2	2	4	6	3	1	2.5		3
B	3	3	5	4	5	4		None	
C	2	2	1	2	3	2			
D	6	5	5	6	8	X			

Find the median and the mode for each situation described.

2. Gwen did 5 speed tests in her typing class. Her times, in minutes, were 2, 3, 2, 5, and 4.

   median time: _____

   mode: _____

3. Ron sold 15 raffle tickets, Jan sold 35, Claudio sold 23, Nunzio sold 47, and Erin sold 23.

   median number of tickets sold: _____

   mode: _____

4. On a math quiz, Jean and her friends got the following scores: 65, 78, 63, 78, 97, 42, and 53.

   median score: _____

   mode: _____

5. Price of a CD at area record stores: $9.50, $12, $14.50, $12, $12.50, $13

   median price: _____

   mode: _____

Find the mean (average) for each set of data.

6. There are 3 women in Jenny's study group. One is 52 years old, one is 29, and one is 39. What is the average age of the women in the study group? _____

7. Nathan asked coworkers how far they traveled from home to work each day. These were the distances reported: 2.5 miles, 4 miles, 9 miles, 3 miles, and 6.5 miles. What was the average distance traveled to get to work? _____

8. These are the amounts Dora spent on grocery bills for the past 6 weeks: $90, $100, $58, $60, $77, and $65. What was the average (mean) amount Dora spent on groceries each week? _____

9. Mrs. Jones tutors 5 students. One is 7 years old, three are 9 years old, and one is 11 years old. What is the average age of Mrs. Jones' students? _____

Working with Graphs

Graphs are used in newspapers, magazines, and even in reports on TV. They present information in picture form to help you read and understand the information quickly. Different types of graphs are used for different purposes. The three types of graphs shown here are the circle graph, the line graph, and the bar graph.

In a **circle graph**, a circle, which represents a whole amount, is divided into slices or wedges. Each slice represents one part of the whole.

A **line graph** uses points or dots to show values. Lines connect the points to show rising or falling values. This type of graph is used to show how data change over time.

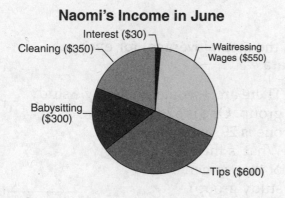

Naomi's Income in June

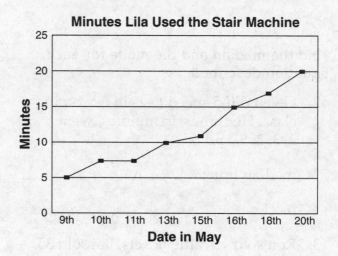

Minutes Lila Used the Stair Machine

A **bar graph** uses thick lines or bars to represent values. Bar graphs make it easy to compare one category with another.

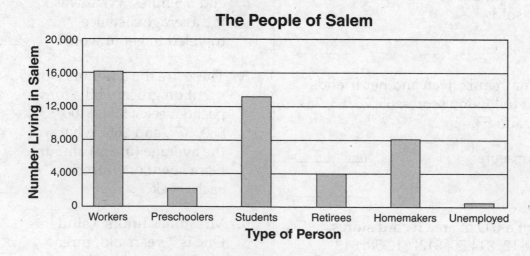

The People of Salem

Reading a Circle Graph

Circle graphs, which are sometimes called pie charts, show a whole that is divided into sections. Each section or "slice" of the circle represents one category of information. The greater the amount being represented, the larger the section or slice. A circle graph makes it easy to compare sections with the whole and with each other. In the circle graph at right, for example, it is very easy to see that the least amount of Naomi's June income came from interest.

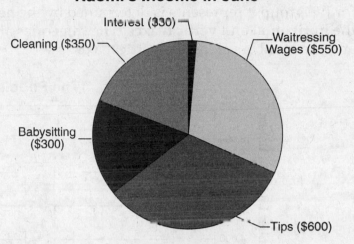

Naomi's Income in June

Interest ($30)
Cleaning ($350)
Waitressing Wages ($550)
Babysitting ($300)
Tips ($600)

PRACTICE

Use the graph above to answer these questions.

1. Approximately what fraction of Naomi's June income came from babysitting?

   A $\frac{1}{2}$ C $\frac{1}{6}$

   B $\frac{2}{3}$ D $\frac{3}{4}$

2. About what fraction of Naomi's June income came from tips?

   F $\frac{1}{5}$ H $\frac{1}{4}$

   G $\frac{1}{3}$ J $\frac{1}{2}$

3. Approximately what part of Naomi's June income was from waitress wages and tips?

   A $\frac{2}{10}$ C $\frac{2}{4}$

   B $\frac{2}{5}$ D $\frac{2}{3}$

4. Which of these made up the greatest amount of Naomi's income in June?

   F cleaning   H interest
   G babysitting   J tips

5. Together, babysitting and tips made up about what fraction of Naomi's June income?

   A $\frac{1}{5}$ C $\frac{1}{4}$

   B $\frac{1}{3}$ D $\frac{1}{2}$

6. What was Naomi's total income in June?

   F $1,830   H $1,650
   G $1,630   J $1,850

7. Did Naomi make more money from tips or from cleaning?

   A tips   B cleaning

8. If Naomi becomes a manager, her wages will double but she will not get any tips. Would she make more money or less money being a manager instead of waiting on tables?

   F more money   G less money

Reading a Bar Graph

A bar graph uses thick lines or bars to represent values. Each bar is labeled, and the number for the group it represents is determined by the height of the bar. Information is found along the **horizontal** and **vertical axes**. The categories are usually found along the horizontal axis and the numbers along the vertical axis.

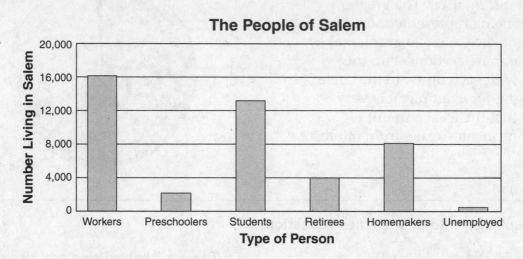

The People of Salem

If the top of a bar does not line up exactly with a number, you can estimate its value. For example, in the graph above, the bar for preschoolers is about halfway between 0 and 4,000. Since 2,000 is equal to half of 4,000, a good estimate for the number of preschoolers is 2,000.

PRACTICE

Use the graph above to answer these questions.

1. Are there more students or homemakers in Salem? _____

2. Which category has the least number of people? _____

3. About how many people living in Salem are retirees? _____

4. Approximately how many more workers are there in Salem than retirees? _____

5. Which of these is the best estimate of the number of students in Salem?

    A 12,000   C 13,000
    B 15,000   D 16,000

6. Approximately how many more retirees than preschoolers are there?

    F 1,000   H 2,000
    G 3,000   J 4,000

7. Which of the following is the closest estimate of the total number of people represented in the graph?

    A 20,000   C   40,000
    B 80,000   D 100,000

8. Who would find this graph most useful?

    F a worker deciding when to retire
    G a person considering whether to open a children's clothing store
    H someone trying to decide the quality of the schools in Salem

Reading a Double Bar Graph

Double bar graphs show a comparison between two or more groups. Each group is represented by a bar of a different color. A key tells what the bars represent.

The graph at right compares the grade-level scores of students before taking a special tutoring class with their scores after taking the tutoring class.

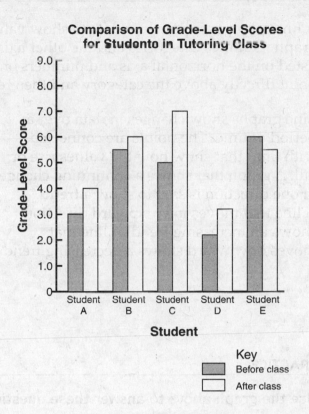

Comparison of Grade-Level Scores for Students in Tutoring Class

Key
Before class
After class

PRACTICE

Use the graph above to answer these questions.

1. What was the grade-level score for Student A before taking the class? _____

2. What was the grade-level score for Student A after taking the class? _____

3. Does Student A's score show an increase or decrease? _____

4. By how much did Student A's score change? _____

5. Which student's grade-level score increased $\frac{1}{2}$ year? _____

6. Which student's score decreased after taking the class? _____

7. Which 2 students showed the same amount of change after taking the class? _____

8. Which student showed the greatest increase in score as a result of taking the class? _____

Reading a Line Graph

A line graph uses points or dots to show values. As in the bar graph, one axis of the line graph identifies categories and the other axis identifies numbers. Categories are usually listed on the horizontal axis and numbers on the vertical axis. To read the graph, find the point directly above the category and then read directly across to find the number.

Line graphs show changes in data over a period of time. The points are connected with lines that show how the values rise or fall. A graph that shows a continuing change in one direction is said to show a **trend**. A line that moves in an upward direction shows an increasing trend. A line that moves downward shows a decreasing trend.

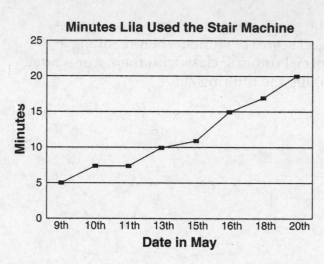

Minutes Lila Used the Stair Machine

PRACTICE

Use the graph above to answer these questions.

1. How many minutes did Lila spend on the stair machine on May 9? _____

2. On which 2 dates did Lila spend the same amount of time on the stair machine? _____

3. How much more time did Lila spend on the stair machine on May 20 than on May 16? _____

4. On which date did Lila spend 3 times as many minutes on the machine as she did May 9? _____

5. By how many minutes did Lila's time on the machine increase from May 13 to May 16? _____

6. Which of these is the best estimate of the average amount of time Lila spent on the stair machine?

   A 5 minutes
   B 8 minutes
   C 12 minutes
   D 17 minutes

7. Which of these best describes what the graph shows?

   F Lila is tired of the machine.
   G Lila is spending more and more time on the stair machine.
   H When Lila is sad, she spends no time on the stair machine.

8. Does the graph show a trend? Explain.

   _____

   _____

Understanding Probability

When we talk about probability, we are talking about how likely it is for something to happen. Words used to describe probability include:

impossible—It cannot happen   equally likely—the chances are the same

not likely—the chances are *not* good   likely—the chances are good

certain—it is sure to happen

Probability can also be expressed with numbers. One way to express probability is as a ratio in fraction form with the number of **possible outcomes** in the denominator, and the number of ways for a **favorable outcome** to occur in the numerator.

Example What is the probability that you will get an even number when you toss a die?

- There are 6 possible outcomes—the numbers 1, 2, 3, 4, 5, or 6.
- Any of 3 favorable outcomes is possible—2, 4, or 6.

$$\frac{\text{favorable outcomes}}{\text{possible outcomes}} = \frac{\text{ways to get an even number}}{\text{different numbers possible}} = \frac{3}{6} = \frac{1}{2}$$

The probability of getting an even number is $\frac{1}{2}$.

PRACTICE

Circle the correct probability.

1. You buy a lottery ticket and win $10 million.

    A impossible   **C** not likely
    B likely   **D** certain

2. Day will follow night.

    F impossible   **H** not likely
    G likely   **J** certain

3. You pick a number from 1–10. The number is greater than 7.

    A $\frac{2}{10}$ or $\frac{1}{5}$ **C** $\frac{3}{10}$

    B $\frac{4}{10}$ or $\frac{2}{5}$ **D** $\frac{5}{10}$ or $\frac{1}{2}$

4. A person is *not* born in a month that begins with the letter *J*.

    F $\frac{1}{12}$ **H** $\frac{3}{12}$ or $\frac{1}{4}$

    G $\frac{6}{12}$ or $\frac{1}{2}$ **J** $\frac{9}{12}$ or $\frac{3}{4}$

Use the spinner for Numbers 5 and 6.

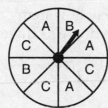

5. You spin the spinner. What is the probability that it will land on D?

    A impossible   **C** not likely
    B likely   **D** certain

6. You spin the spinner. What is the probability that it will land on A?

    F $\frac{1}{8}$ **H** $\frac{2}{8}$ or $\frac{1}{4}$

    G $\frac{3}{8}$ **J** $\frac{4}{8}$ or $\frac{1}{2}$

Data Interpretation Skills Checkup

This circle graph shows the form of transportation people used to travel on vacation. Use the graph to answer Questions 1–3.

How People Traveled on Vacation

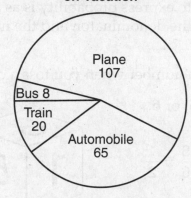

Hakim sells appliances 5 days each week. Use the graph of his sales last week to answer Questions 4–6.

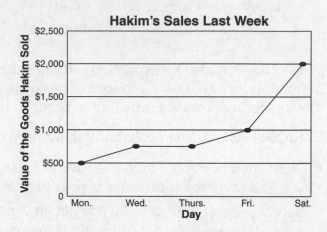

1. What form of transportation did the greatest number of people in the survey use?

   A train   **C** plane
   B automobile **D** bus

2. Approximately how many times as many people drove as traveled by train?

   F 5   **H** 4
   G 3   **J** 2

3. How did the fewest number of people travel?

   A train   **C** plane
   B automobile **D** bus

4. What was the difference in the value of Hakim's sales on Monday and Saturday?

   F $ 500   **H** $1,000
   G $1,500   **J** $2,500

5. Which is the best estimate of Hakim's average sales per day last week?

   A $ 500   **C** $ 600
   B $1,000   **D** $1,750

6. Which of the following can you tell from the graph?

   F Hakim is a good salesman.
   G The value of Hakim's sales increased throughout the week.
   H Hakim works very long hours.

This graph shows the population of major cities in the United States. Study the graph and then answer Questions 7–9.

Population of Major U.S. Cities
in 2004

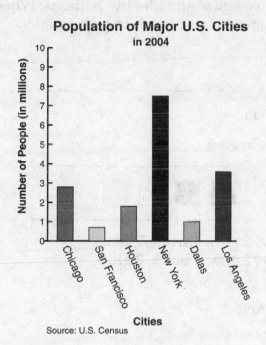

Source: U.S. Census

7. Which of the cities shown have a population of 1 million or fewer people?

A Los Angeles and Dallas
B San Francisco and Dallas
C Houston and Dallas
D San Francisco and Houston

8. Approximately how many more people live in Houston than in Dallas?

F 0.2 million   H 0.6 million
G 1 million   J 2 million

9. What is the median population of the cities shown?

A 2.3 million   C 2.6 million
B 2.8 million   D 2.9 million

Use the spinner shown below to answer Questions 10–13. Circle the letter that best describes the probability described when the spinner is spun.

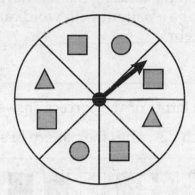

10. The spinner will land on a square instead of a circle.

F impossible   H equally likely
G more likely   J certain

11. The spinner will land on a star.

A impossible   C equally likely
B more likely   D certain

12. The spinner will land on a circle.

F $\frac{1}{3}$ H $\frac{1}{2}$
G $\frac{2}{3}$ J $\frac{1}{4}$

13. The spinner will land on a square.

A $\frac{1}{4}$ C $\frac{1}{8}$
B $\frac{1}{2}$ D $\frac{1}{3}$

Algebra

Identifying Geometric Patterns

A key to understanding math is having the ability to recognize and identify patterns. When you describe a pattern with words and symbols, you are using a branch of mathematics called **algebra**.

PRACTICE

Circle the letter of the correct answer for each question.

1. Which describes the pattern of squares in the box below?

   A 1 white, 1 gray, 1 white, 1 black   C 1 white, 2 gray, 1 white, 2 black
   B 1 white, 2 gray, 2 white, 2 black   D 1 white, 2 gray, 1 black, 2 gray

2. Which square should come next in the pattern above?

   F   G ▨   H ■

3. Which describes the pattern in the box below?

   A point up, point down   C point up, point right, point down, point right
   B point up, point right   D point up, point right, point down, point left

4. Which is the missing shape in the box above?

   F ▲   G ▶   H ▼

5. Which names the number of equal parts in the two missing figures?

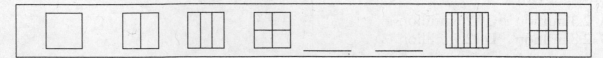

   A 3 and 5   C 4 and 5
   B 5 and 6   D 5 and 7

6. Describe the pattern in the box below.

7. Circle the letter of the missing figure in the pattern above.

A   B   C

8. Draw the two figures that are missing from the pattern below.

9. Draw the figure that is missing from the pattern below.

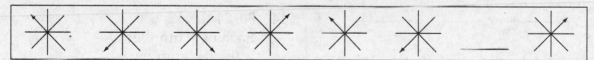

10. Draw the two figures that are missing from the pattern below.

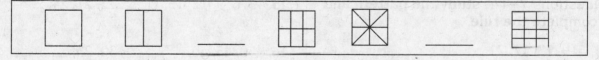

11. Draw the two figures that are missing from the pattern below.

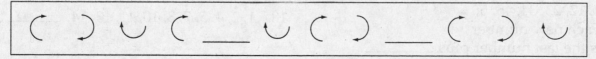

Identifying Number Patterns

You can create patterns with numbers as well as with shapes.

PRACTICE

For Questions 1–6, fill in the missing numbers to continue the pattern.

1. Start with 16.
   Count back by 3.

   16, 13, 10, _____, _____, _____

2. Start with 3.
   Add 6.

   3, 9, 15, _____, _____, _____

3. Start with 3.
   Add 5.

   3, 8, 13, _____, _____, _____

4. Start with 2.
   Multiply by 2.

   2, 4, 8, _____, _____, _____

5. Start with 1.
   Multiply by 2, then add 1.

   1, 3, 7, _____, _____, _____

6. Start with 7.
   Multiply by 3, then subtract 1.

   7, 20, 59, _____, _____, _____

For Questions 7–14, study the pattern and then complete the rule.

7. 1, 5, 9, 13, 17, 21
   Each new number
   is the last number plus _____.

8. 1, 12, 23, 34, 45, 56
   Each new number
   is the last number plus _____.

9. 25, 22, 19, 16, 13, 10
   Each new number
   is the last number minus _____.

10. 1, 3, 9, 27, 81
    Each new number
    is the last number times _____.

11. 0, 7, 14, 21, 28
    Each new number
    is the last number _____.

12. 15, 30, 45, 60, 75, 90
    Each new number
    is the last number _____.

13. 29, 24, 19, 14, 9, 4
    Each new number
    is the last number _____.

14. 30, 24, 18, 12, 6, 0
    Each new number
    is the last number _____.

For Questions 15–19, write the missing number or numbers.

15. 3, 6, 9, 12, 15, _____, 21, 24, 27

16. 50, 45, 40, _____, 30, 25, _____, 15

17. 1, 2, 2, 3, 4, 4, 5, 6, 6, 7, 8, _____

18. 1, 2, 4, 5, 7, 8, 10, 11, 13, 14, _____

19. 1, 3, 2, 4, 3, 5, 4, 6, 5, _____

Analyzing Relationships in Number Sentences

The number sentences below are incomplete. Use what you know about number facts to answer each question

PRACTICE

Write +, −, ×, or ÷ in the circle to make each number sentence true.

Example $2 \oplus 3 = 5$

1. $4 \bigcirc 6 = 10$

2. $5 \bigcirc 3 = 2$

3. $9 \bigcirc 3 = 27$

4. $1 \bigcirc 9 = 10$

5. $11 \bigcirc 7 = 18$

6. $27 \bigcirc 5 = 22$

7. $35 \bigcirc 5 = 7$

8. $12 \bigcirc 6 = 2$

9. $13 \bigcirc 13 = 26$

10. $156 \bigcirc 16 = 140$

11. $54 \bigcirc 9 = 6$

12. $7 \bigcirc 8 = 56$

Write the number that makes each number sentence true. You can use related facts to help find missing numbers.

Example $47 - \square = 25$
Think: $47 - 25 = \square$

13. $3 + \square = 7$

14. $5 + \square = 13$

15. $9 + \square = 19$

16. $33 + \square = 45$

17. $12 - \square = 8$

18. $15 - \square = 6$

19. $52 - \square = 40$

20. $75 - \square = 53$

21. $7 \times \square = 14$

22. $6 \times \square = 60$

23. $5 \times \square = 60$

24. $51 \div \square = 17$

Reviewing Basic Number Properties

Earlier in this book, you learned some properties that apply to working with numbers. In algebra, letters of the alphabet, or **variables**, take the place of numbers, but the same properties apply. Each rule is shown here with numbers and with variables.

Note: Any letter can be used as a variable.

Properties of Zero

- If you add or subtract zero, the amount does not change.

  Addition: $15 + 0 = 15$ Subtraction: $15 - 0 = 15$

  $n + 0 = n$ $n - 0 = n$

- If you subtract a number from itself, the remainder will be zero.

  $27 - 27 = 0$ $m - m = 0$

- If you multiply any amount by zero, the product will be zero.

  $0 \times 12 = 0$ $0 \times b = 0$

- If you divide zero by any nonzero number, the quotient will be zero.

  $0 \div 5 = 0$ $0 \div n = 0$

- You *cannot* divide by zero. Each division must have a related multiplication. There can be no related multiplication for dividing by zero.

  $15 \div 5 = 3$ and $3 \times 5 = 15$ But, $5 \div 0 = ?$ There is no number $\times$ 0 that equals 5.

Properties of One

- If you multiply or divide a number by 1, the value does not change.

  Multiplication: $25 \times 1 = 25$ Division: $25 \div 1 = 25$

  $r \times 1 = r$ $y \div 1 = y$

- If you divide a number by itself, the quotient will be 1.

  $42 \div 42 = 1$ $n \div n = 1$

Changing the Order of the Numbers (The Commutative Property)

- Changing the order of the numbers *does not* change the result in addition or multiplication.

  Addition: $4 + 5 = 9$ and $5 + 4 = 9$ Multiplication: $4 \times 5 = 20$ and $5 \times 4 = 20$

  $x + y = z$ and $y + x = z$ $x \times y = w$ and $y \times x = w$

  $x + y = y + x$ $x \times y = y \times x$

- Changing the order of the numbers *does* change the result in subtraction and division.

  Subtraction: $8 - 5 = 3$ but $5 - 8 \neq 3$ Division: $30 \div 3 = 10$, but $3 \div 30 \neq 10$

  $a - b = c$ but $b - a \neq c$ $m \div n = p$, but $n \div m \neq p$

  $a - b \neq b - a$ $m \div n \neq n \div m$

Grouping the Numbers (The Associative Property)

- In both addition and multiplication, if there are more than two numbers, you can change the way you group them and the sum or product will be the same.

Addition:	$(3 + 4) + 5 = 3 + (4 + 5)$	Multiplication:	$(5 \times 6) \times 7 = 5 \times (6 \times 7)$
	$7 + 5 = 3 + 9$		$30 \times 7 = 5 \times 42$
	$12 = 12$		$210 = 210$
	$(a + b) + c = a + (b + c)$		$(a \times b) \times c = a \times (b \times c)$

- In subtraction and division, the answer will *not* be the same if you change the way you group the numbers.

Subtraction:	$(8 - 4) - 1 \neq 8 - (4 - 1)$	Division:	$(27 \div 9) \div 3 \neq 27 \div (9 \div 3)$
	$4 - 1 \neq 8 - 3$		$3 \div 3 \neq 27 \div 3$
	$3 \neq 5$		$1 \neq 9$
	$(a - b) - c \neq a - (b - c)$		$(a \div b) \div c \neq a \div (b \div c)$

Opposite or Inverse Operations

- Addition and subtraction are inverse operations. One can be used to undo the other.

$3 + 5 = 8$	$8 - 5 = 3$	and	$15 - 6 = 9$	$9 + 6 = 15$
$a + b = c$	$c - b = a$		$x - y = w$	$w + y = x$

- Multiplication and division are inverse operations. One can be used to undo the other.

$27 \div 3 = 9$	$3 \times 9 = 27$	and	$8 \times 5 = 40$	$40 \div 5 = 8$
$q \div p = k$	$k \times p = q$		$g \times h = m$	$m \div h = g$

PRACTICE

Fill in the missing operation sign and/or number to make each sentence true.

1. $123 \bigcirc 123 = 1$

2. $14 \bigcirc 14 = 0$

3. $0 \bigcirc 32 = 32$

4. $520 \div \square = 1$

5. $n \times 0 = \square$

6. $m \div \square = m$

7. $y - 0 = \square$

Circle *T* if the statement is true or *F* if the statement is false.

8. $7 \times 8 = 56$, so $8 \times 7 = 56$ T   F

9. $39 \div 3 = 13$, so $13 \div 3 = 39$ T   F

10. $54 \div 9 = 6$, so $54 \div 6 = 9$ T   F

11. $12 + 9 + 3 = 3 + 12 + 9$ T   F

12. $(a \times b) \times c = a \times (b \times c)$ T   F

13. $50 - (25 - 5) = (50 - 25) - 5$ T   F

14. $2 \times 3 \times 10 = 10 \times 2 \times 3$ T   F

Working with Functions

Imagine a machine you can put numbers into. The machine has a rule, or **function**, that creates a new value for each number that is put into it. The machine applies the rule to the number and gives out the result. The number that comes out depends on the number that is put in.

Example   The rule is *Add 4*.

In	0	1	2	3	4
Out	4	5	6	7	8

PRACTICE

Use the function, or rule, and write the missing numbers to complete each table.

1. Subtract 5.

In	10	20	40		80
Out	5		35	50	

2. Multiply by 3.

In	4	10	9		100
Out		30	27	9	

3. Multiply by 2, then subtract 1.

In	0	1	2	3
Out		1	3	19

Circle the letter of the function, or rule, that describes the pattern.

4.

In	0	1	2	3	4
Out	4	5	6	7	8

   A Add 1, then multiply by 2.
   B Multiply by 5, then subtract 1.
   C Add 4.

5.

In	10	20	30	40	50
Out	32	62	92	122	152

   F Add 30.
   G Add 40, then subtract 8.
   H Multiply by 3, then add 2.

Write the function, or rule, that will change each *In* number to the corresponding *Out* number.

6.

In	3	4	5	6	7
Out	1	2	3	4	5

_____

7.

In	2	4	6	8	10
Out	12	14	16	18	20

_____

8.

In	0	3	5	7	9
Out	0	15	25	35	45

_____

9.

In	4	12	8	10	35
Out	16	24	20	22	47

_____

10.

In	48	92	24	192	56
Out	12	23	6	48	14

_____

Writing Algebraic Expressions

An **expression** is a combination of numbers, variables, and operation signs that make up part of a complete sentence. A **variable** is a letter or symbol that takes the place of a number in an expression or math sentence.

You can use an algebraic expression to describe a situation.

Example   At the Acme Company, workers are paid their regular hourly wage plus an additional $5 for each hour of overtime.

- Let a variable, such as h, stand for the hourly wage.
- Add 5 to the hourly wage to represent the overtime wage. $h + 5$

The situation described can be represented with the expression $h + 5$.

PRACTICE

Circle the letter of the expression that matches the words.

1. a number increased by 32

   A $n - 32$ **C** $n \times 32$
   B $n \div 32$ **D** $n + 32$

2. five less than a number

   F $n - 5$ **H** $5 - n$
   G $\dfrac{n}{5}$ **J** $5 \times n$

3. three times a number

   A $3 + n$ **C** $3 \times n$
   B $\dfrac{n}{3}$ **D** $n - 3$

4. $\dfrac{2}{3}$ of a number

   F $\dfrac{2}{3} + n$ **H** $\dfrac{2}{3} - n$
   G $\dfrac{2}{3} \times n$ **J** $n \div \dfrac{2}{3}$

Write an algebraic expression for each phrase. Let the letter n stand for the unknown number.

5. the sum of a number and twenty-four   _____

6. six more than a number   _____

7. seven less than a number   _____

8. half of a number   _____

9. the sum of a number and eight   _____

10. the product of a number and six   _____

11. thirteen divided by a number   _____

12. a number decreased by six   _____

13. a number multiplied by fourteen   _____

14. a number increased by ten   _____

Writing Algebraic Expressions (continued)

Writing an algebraic expression to describe relationships in a word problem is a useful strategy for problem solving. Often, the first letter of the word represented by the variable is used in the expression. For example, h might represent a number of hours, d might represent a number of desks, and so on.

Example Jack earns an hourly wage. Starting next month, he will earn $2 more per hour. What will his new hourly wage be?

Let w represent Jack's hourly wage. His new wage will be $w + 2$ dollars.

PRACTICE

Write an algebraic expression to describe each situation.

15. Let r stand for the rent Max now pays each month. Starting next month, Max will pay 20 dollars more per month. What will his new monthly rent payment be?

    _____

16. There are p pieces in an extra large pizza. If 4 friends evenly divide an extra large pizza, how many pieces will each friend get?

    _____

17. Loraine makes x dollars a month. Each month $450 is taken out of her paycheck for taxes. What is Loraine's monthly take-home pay?

    _____

18. Rock candy costs c cents a pound. What is the cost of 3 pounds of rock candy?

    _____

19. In the talent show, there will be d dancers and m musicians. How many performers will there be in all?

    _____

20. There will be k skaters in the competition. Each skater will perform for exactly 4 minutes. What is the total amount of time that the skaters will be performing?

    _____

21. There were 28 students enrolled in Elise's class, but d students dropped out. How many students are in the class now?

    _____

22. Karen needs 6 cups of flour, but she has only f cups of flour. How many more cups of flour does Karen need?

    _____

23. When Kay last saw Joe, he was 7 years old. Now he is y years old. How long has it been since Kay saw Joe?

    _____

24. Maria weighed 172 pounds right before her baby was born. Afterward, she weighed x pounds. How much weight did she lose when her baby was born?

    _____

Evaluating Expressions

The value of an expression depends on the value(s) assigned to the variable(s) it contains. To **evaluate**, or find the value of an expression, replace the variable with the value it represents.

Examples

Find the value of $n + 8$.
- Let $n = 6$.

  $n + 8 = 6 + 8 = 14$

  $n + 8 = 14$

- Let $n = 12$.

  $n + 8 = 12 + 8 = 20$

  $n + 8 = 20$

Find the value of $(3 \times n) - 5$.
- Let $n = 4$.

  $(3 \times n) - 5 = (3 \times 4) - 5 = 12 - 5 = 7$

  $(3 \times n) - 5 = 7$

- Let $n = 15$.

  $(3 \times n) - 5 = (3 \times 15) - 5 = 45 - 5 = 40$

  $3n - 5 = 40$

PRACTICE

Circle the letter of the correct answer.

1. What is the value of the expression $4 + (6 \times m)$ when $m = 4$?

   A 14   C 40

   B 24   D 28

2. What is the value of the expression $(32 - y) + 5$ when $y = 7$?

   F 30   H 20

   G 27   J 37

3. What is the value of the expression $\frac{n}{4}$ when $n = 64$?

   A 16   C 256

   B 60   D 21

4. What is the value of the expression $3 \times \frac{p}{6}$ when $p = 100$?

   F 30   H 50

   G 70   J 90

5. What is the value of the expression $7n + 4$ when $n = 5$?

   A 14   C 39

   B 19   D 54

Evaluate each expression. Use the values shown below for the variables.

$n = 1$ $a = 2$ $x = 3$ $y = 5$

6. $a \times y =$ _____

7. $4 \times a =$ _____

8. $x + (y \times a) =$ _____

9. $y \times n =$ _____

10. $10 \times \frac{y}{a} =$ _____

11. $(a + x) - n =$ _____

12. $y + (8 \div a) =$ _____

13. $(4 \times y) - x =$ _____

14. $4 \times (y - x) =$ _____

Using Equations

An **equation** is a mathematical sentence that uses an equal sign to show that two amounts are equal. Examples of equations include:

$$x = 30 \qquad m = 43 - 9 \qquad 17 + 8 = 25 \qquad (4 \times y) + 12 = 92$$

You can write an equation that represents the situation to help you solve a word problem.

Example   Terrence just bought 3 new wrenches. He now has a total of 15 wrenches. How many wrenches did Terrence have to begin with?

- Use a letter to name the unknown.
  In this problem you need to find how many wrenches Terrence had to begin with. Let w stand for the wrenches he had to begin with.

- Describe the situation. Look for signal words that can help.
  The problem says *He now has a total of 15 wrenches.* Use addition to find the total. The number of wrenches Terrence had to begin with (w) plus the number he bought (3) totals 15.

- Write an equation to represent the situation. $w + 3 = 15$

PRACTICE

For Numbers 1–3, circle the equation that can be used to solve the problem.

1. A month ago, Cecelia had 7 pairs of shoes. Now she has 12 pairs. How many pairs of shoes has she bought in the past month? (Let p = shoes bought)

   A $7 + 12 = p$ **C** $p - 7 = 12$
   B $7 + p = 12$ **D** $12 \div 7 = p$

2. Howard bought 5 big bags of potato chips. Now there are $1\frac{1}{2}$ bags left. How many bags of potato chips have been eaten? (Let b = bags of chips eaten)

   F $b - 5 = 1\frac{1}{2}$ **H** $b + 5 = 1\frac{1}{2}$
   G $b - 1\frac{1}{2} = 5$ **J** $5 - b = 1\frac{1}{2}$

3. Tricia is 15 years older than her cousin. When her cousin is 65 years of age, how old will Tricia be? (Let t = Tricia)

   F $t \times 15 = 65$ **H** $t + 15 = 65$
   G $15 + 65 = t$ **J** $65 - t = 15$

For Numbers 4–6, write an equation to describe the problem. Use the letter x for the unknown. You do not need to solve.

4. Rochelle had 24 bags of used clothes. She gave 7 of the bags to a charity. How many bags are left?

   _____

5. There are 12,000 people living in Bloomington. Ten years ago, the population was 9,000 people. How much has the population grown in the past 10 years?

   _____

6. Clarice worked at her first job for 3 years. Then she worked at Available Temps for 7 years. How many years did she work in all?

   _____

Using Addition and Subtraction to Solve Equations

When you solve an equation, you find the value of the variable. You might be able to solve simple equations in your head, but when equations get more complicated, it is important to have a procedure to follow.

Think of amounts that are balanced on a scale, as in Figure A. If you add something to one side of the scale, you need to add the same amount to the other side to keep it balanced (Figure B). By the same token, if you remove or subtract something from one side, you have to remove or subtract the same amount from the other side to keep the balance (Figure C).

Figure A	Figure B	Figure C
$x \quad 10$	$x+4 \quad 10+4$	$x-8 \quad 10-8$
$x = 10$	$x + 4 = 10 + 4$	$x - 8 = 10 - 8$

To solve some equations, you need to subtract the amount that was added to the variable. Be sure to subtract on both sides of the equation.

Example Solve $x + 3 = 15$.

- 3 has been added to x. Subtract 3 to leave only x.
- Subtract 3 from both sides of the equation to keep the balance.

$$x = 12$$

$$\begin{array}{rcl} x + 3 &=& 15 \\ -3 &=& -3 \\ \hline x + 0 &=& 12 \\ x &=& 12 \end{array}$$

Check your answer.
Replace the variable in the original equation with the value you found. You should get a true sentence.

Check
$12 + 3 = 15$

Sometimes you need to add an amount that was subtracted from the variable.

Example Solve $x - 18 = 27$.

- 18 has been subtracted from x. Add 18 to have all of x with nothing subtracted.
- Add 18 on both sides of the equation to keep the balance.

$$x = 45$$

$$\begin{array}{rcl} x - 18 &=& 27 \\ +18 &=& +18 \\ \hline x + 0 &=& 45 \\ x &=& 45 \end{array}$$

Check your answer.
Replace the variable in the original equation with the value you found.

Check
$45 - 18 = 27$

PRACTICE

Solve each equation. Then check to see whether your solution makes the original equation true.

1. $x + 12 = 20$ $x = $ _____

2. $x + 44 = 69$ $x = $ _____

3. $9 + 6 = x$ $x = $ _____

4. $x - 13 = 12$ $x = $ _____

5. $45 - 6 = x$ $x = $ _____

6. $x + 14 = 54$ $x = $ _____

7. $x + 32 = 47$ $x = $ _____

8. $x - 39 = 64$ $x = $ _____

Algebra Skills Checkup

Circle the letter for the correct answer to each question.

1. What value of n makes both equations true?

$$4 + n = 16$$
$$16 - n = 4$$

   A 4   **C** 8
   B 13   **D** 12

2. If $8 \times n = 48$, then n is

   F 40   **H** 6
   G 4   **J** 52

3. What rule will change each *In* number to the corresponding *Out* number?

In	3	2	5	8
Out	12	10	16	22

   A Add 3, then multiply by 2.
   B Multiply by 3, then add 3.
   C Multiply by 4.
   D Add 9.

4. What number is missing from this number pattern?

   56, 50, 44, 38, 32, _____, 20, 14

   F 26   **H** 24
   G 22   **J** 28

5. Which group of numbers is missing from this number pattern?

   9, 12, 15, _____, _____, _____, 27, 30, 33

   A 17, 19, 21   **C** 17, 20, 23
   B 18, 21, 24   **D** 18, 22, 24

6. Which number sentence *does not* have 5 as a solution?

   F $5 - 1 = \square$
   G $5 \times 1 = \square$
   H $5 \div 1 = \square$
   J $5 - 0 = \square$

7. Which operation sign goes in the circle to make the number sentence true?

$$9 \bigcirc 9 = 1$$

   A +   **C** ×
   B −   **D** ÷

8. How many squares will be in the next entry in the pattern below?

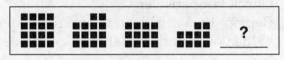

   F 6   **H** 8
   G 10   **J** 12

9. What is the value of $3 + (n \times 4)$ when $n = 5$?

   A 18   **C** 20
   B 23   **D** 27

10. If $80 \div x = 8$, what is the value of x?

   F 10   **H** 72
   G 11   **J** 5

11. Which describes the pattern of Xs and Os?

   X X O X X O X X O

   A 1 X, then 1 O
   B 2 Xs, then 2 Os
   C 2 Xs, then 1 O
   D 1 X, then 2 Os

12. Which describes the number pattern?

$$1, 5, 9, 13, 17, 21, 25$$

   F Add 4 to the last number.
   G Add 3 to the last number.
   H Count by fives.
   J Multiply the last number by 5.

13. Jason spent $33 on theater tickets. He bought 4 tickets. Which of these equations shows how to find the cost (c) of each ticket?

   A $c = 33 \times 4$
   B $c = 33 - 4$
   C $c = 33 + 4$
   D $c = 33 \div 4$

14. What sign goes in the circle to make this equation true?

$$6 \bigcirc 3 = 2$$

   F $+$ H $-$
   G $\times$ J $\div$

15. This list shows the wages given to laborers at a construction company.

Experience	Hourly Wage
None	$5.10
1 year	$5.40
2 years	$5.70
3 years	$6.00
4 years	$6.30

What pattern, if any, is shown in the list?

   A Wages double with every year of experience.
   B Wages increase 30 cents an hour with every year of experience.
   C The more experience a laborer has, the larger his or her raises.
   D There is no pattern in the list.

16. Brad bought a sandwich for $4.50 and a drink for $1.25 for lunch. With tax, the total bill was $6.25. Which of these equations shows how much tax (t) he paid?

   F $t - (\$6.25 \quad \$4.50) + \$1.25$
   G $t - \$6.25 = \$4.50 + \$1.25$
   H $t = \$6.25 - (\$4.50 + \$1.25)$
   J $t = (\$6.25 - \$4.50) + \$1.25$

17. Which statement is *not* true?

   A $3 + (6 + y) = (3 + 6) + y$
   B $4 + 12 + 8 = 4 + 8 + 12$
   C $40 \div (10 \div 2) = (40 \div 10) \div 2$
   D $x + y = y + x$

18. Which is the correct algebraic expression for the phrase shown?

   9 increased by a number p

   F $9 \times p$
   G $9 \div p$
   H $9 + p$
   J $9 - p$

19. If $m - 120 = 30$, what is the value of m?

   A 360
   B 50
   C 40
   D 150

20. What numbers belong in the boxes?

In	100	80	60	20	12
Out	25	20	15		

   F 10 and 5
   G 5 and 3
   H 8 and 6
   J 12 and 9

Measurement

Understanding Measurement

The **customary system**, or English system of measurement, is used in the United States. Most countries in the rest of the world use the **metric system**. Different types of measurement and common units used in both systems are listed below.

Type of Measurement	Commonly Used Units of Measure	
	Customary System	Metric System
Length The distance from one end to the other. Includes height, width, and depth.	inches, feet, yards, miles	millimeters, centimeters, kilometers Meters are the basic unit.
Weight/Mass How heavy something is. In the metric system, the term *mass* is used instead of *weight*.	ounces, pounds, tons	milligrams, centigrams, kilograms Grams are the basic unit.
Capacity The amount of matter something can hold	pints, quarts, gallons, fluid ounces	milliliters, centiliters, kiloliters Liters are the basic unit.
Volume The amount of space something occupies	cubic inches, cubic feet, cubic yards, cubic miles	cubic meters/millimeters, centimeters, kilometers
Area The size of a surface	square inches, square feet, square yards, square miles	square meters/millimeters, centimeters, kilometers
Temperature A measure of heat	degrees Fahrenheit (°F)	degrees Celsius (°C)

PRACTICE

Identify the type of measurement that would be used for the situation. Then circle the units that might be used to measure it. The first one has been done for you.

1. coffee poured in a restaurant   <u>capacity</u>   pounds   (gallons)   yards

2. distance between two cities   _____   miles   degrees   pints

3. size of a lawn   _____   miles   quarts   square feet

4. amount of gasoline a tank holds   _____   pounds   gallons   degrees

5. amount of cheese to buy   _____   degrees   quarts   ounces

6. setting the oven to bake a cake   _____   ounces   degrees   pints

7. distance a person swims   _____   yards   ounces   square feet

8. number of boxes that will fit in the closet   _____   cubic feet   degrees   square feet

Choosing an Appropriate Unit of Measure

You would not measure the distance between New York and Florida in inches, nor would you use an eyedropper to fill a swimming pool. The information below relates units of measure with familiar objects. It can help you decide the best unit to use.

Customary Units	Metric Units
Weight	**Mass**
pencil ≈ 1 ounce	sewing needle ≈ 1 milligram
package of hot dogs ≈ 1 pound	paper clip ≈ 1 gram
automobile ≈ about 1 ton	6 apples ≈ 1 kilogram
Length	**Length**
small paper clip ≈ 1 inch	thickness of a dime ≈ 1 millimeter
man's foot ≈ 1 foot	width of your baby finger ≈ 1 centimeter
height of a doorknob ≈ 1 yard	length of a baseball bat ≈ 1 meter
Capacity	**Capacity**
coffee cup ≈ 1 cup	medicine dropper ≈ 1 milliliter
tall bottle of soda ≈ 1 quart	tall bottle of soda ≈ 1 liter
large bottle of milk ≈ 1 gallon	5 bathtubs of water ≈ 1 kiloliter

Note: ≈ means *approximately equal to*

PRACTICE

Circle the better unit to measure each one.

1. the mass of a wristwatch
   A grams
   B kilograms

2. the weight of a bicycle
   C ounces
   D pounds

3. the amount of water in a fish tank
   E milliliters
   F liters

4. the height of a tall building
   G feet
   H yards

5. the width of a picture
   A centimeters
   B kilometers

Circle the most reasonable estimate.

6. the weight of a bag of popcorn
   F 6 oz   H 60 oz
   G 6 lb   J 60 lb

7. the amount of water to fill a bathtub
   A 1.3 L   C 13 L
   B 130 L   D 1,300 L

8. the height of a refrigerator
   F $5\frac{1}{2}$ in.   H $5\frac{1}{2}$ ft
   G $5\frac{1}{2}$ yd   J $5\frac{1}{2}$ mi

9. the length of a room
   A 10 mm   C 10 m
   B 10 cm   D 10 km

Converting Units Within the Customary System

The same length can be described in different units. For example, a person might say she is 60 inches tall, or she might say she is 5 feet tall. To **convert**, or change, from one unit to another, as from inches to feet, or from cups to pints, you need to know the exchange rate between the units. Common equivalent measures within the customary system are shown below.

Length	Weight	Capacity
12 inches (in.) = 1 foot (ft)	16 ounces (oz) = 1 pound (lb)	8 fluid ounces (fl oz) = 1 cup (c)
3 feet = 1 yard (yd)	2,000 pounds = 1 ton (T)	2 cups = 1 pint (pt)
36 inches = 1 yard		2 pints = 1 quart (qt)
5,280 feet = 1 mile (mi)		4 quarts = 1 gallon (gal)

Time	
60 seconds (sec) = 1 minute (min)	365 days = 1 year (yr)
60 minutes = 1 hour (hr)	4 weeks = 1 month (mo)
24 hours = 1 day (d)	12 months = 1 year
7 days = 1 week (wk)	52 weeks = 1 year

One way to convert units is to use multiplication or division.

• Multiply to convert larger units to smaller units.

Example   2 ft = _____ in.
• Identify the exchange rate.   1 ft = 12 in.
• Multiply each foot by 12. $2 \times 12 = 24$
       2 ft = 24 in.

• Divide to convert smaller units to larger units.

Example   14 wks = _____ mo
• Identify the exchange rate.   4 wks = 1 mo
• Divide the number of weeks by 4. $14 \div 4 = 3$ R2
  3 R2 represents 3 months and 2 weeks. The remainder can also be written as $\frac{2}{4}$ or $\frac{1}{2}$.
      14 wks = 3 months 2 weeks or $3\frac{1}{2}$ months

PRACTICE

Multiply or divide to convert each measurement.

1. 7 T = _____ lb

2. 45 ft = _____ yd

3. 72 in. = _____ ft

4. 8 c = _____ pt

5. 8 oz = _____ lb

6. 240 min = _____ hr

7. 91 d = _____ wk

8. 2 ft = _____ yd

9. 1 wk = _____ hr

10. 12 pt = _____ qt

Another way to convert units is to set up a proportion.

Example   6 yd = _____ ft

- Write a ratio with the exchange rate of yards to feet. $\dfrac{yd}{ft}$ $\dfrac{1}{3}$
- Write an equal ratio to create a proportion.
  Use the amount you want to convert for the second ratio. $\dfrac{yd}{ft}$ $\dfrac{1}{3} = \dfrac{6}{n}$
  Let a variable represent the amount you do not know.

- Find cross products and solve for the missing number. $1 \times n = 3 \times 6$

Since the variable represents feet, the 18 is 18 feet. $n = 18$

        6 yd = 18 ft

Sometimes more than one step is needed. For example, to get from gallons to cups, you can first go from gallons to quarts, and then from quarts to cups.

Example   2 gal = _____ c   gallons to quarts   →   quarts to cups

- Set up a proportion. $\dfrac{gal}{qt}$ $\dfrac{1}{4} = \dfrac{2}{n}$ $\dfrac{qt}{c}$ $\dfrac{1}{4} = \dfrac{8}{n}$

- Cross multiply. $1 \times n = 2 \times 4$ $1 \times n = 4 \times 8$
                      $n = 8$ $n = 32$

- Solve.   2 gal = 8 qt   →   8 qt = 32 c

        2 gal = 32 c

PRACTICE

Use a proportion to convert each measurement.

11. 5 yd = _____ ft	17. 6 hr = _____ sec
12. 3 T = _____ lb	18. 245 d = _____ wk
13. 6 in. = _____ ft	19. 6 lb = _____ oz
14. 36 fl oz = _____ c	20. 1 ft = _____ yd
15. 4 yd = _____ in.	21. 3 qt = _____ pt
16. 18 in. = _____ ft	22. 250 lb = _____ T

Converting Units Within the Metric System

The metric system is based on groups of ten. This system is easy to use because it works very much like our decimal system.

In the metric system the basic unit of length is the meter (m), the basic unit of mass is the gram (g), and the basic unit of capacity is the liter (L). Amounts that are greater than or less than a basic unit are identified with prefixes. The same prefixes are used with each type of unit.

- Prefixes for amounts less than the basic unit:
  deci (d) = one tenth of the basic unit
  cent (c) = one one-hundredth of the basic unit
  milli (m) = one one-thousandth of the basic unit

- Prefixes for amounts greater than the basic unit:
  deka (dk) = ten units
  hecto (h) = one hundred units
  kilo (k) = one thousand units

1,000	100	10	1	0.1	0.01	0.001
kilo (k)	hecto (h)	deka (dk)	basic unit	deci (d)	centi (c)	milli (m)
km	hm	dkm	meter (m)	dm	cm	mm
kL	hL	dkL	liter (L)	dL	cL	mL
kg	hg	dkg	gram (g)	dg	cg	mg

Just as in the customary system, to convert units within the metric system you need to know the conversion or exchange rates. For example, 1 kilogram = 1,000 g.

PRACTICE

Write the equivalent for each metric measure.

1. 1 m = _____ cm
2. 1 km = _____ m
3. 100 cg = _____ g

4. 100 cL = _____ L
5. 1 hg = _____ g
6. 1 kL = _____ L

7. 10 cm = _____ dm
8. 1 m = _____ mm
9. 1,000 g = _____ kg

You can use proportions to convert metric units.

Example   85 cg = _____ g

- Set up a ratio using the basic exchange rate.
- Write a proportion.
  Use a variable for the amount you need to find.

$$\frac{cg}{g} \quad \frac{100}{1}$$

$$\frac{cg}{g} \quad \frac{100}{1} = \frac{85}{n}$$

- Cross multiply.

$$100 \times n = 85$$

- Divide by 100 on both sides of the equal sign.

Cancel on the left side.

$$\frac{{}^{1}\cancel{100}n}{\cancel{100}_{1}} = \frac{85}{100}$$

- Write the fraction as a decimal. Metric units are always written as decimals.

$$\frac{85}{100} = 0.85$$

$$85 \text{ cg} = 0.85 \text{ g}$$

Another way to convert is to use multiplication or division. A place-value chart can help.

• Multiply to convert larger units to smaller units.

Example   5 hm = _____ dm

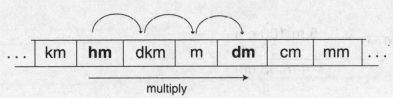

| ... | km | **hm** | dkm | m | **dm** | cm | mm | ... |

multiply

• Find **hecto**meters in the chart. **Deci**meters are three columns to the right. Each column represents a power of 10; 3 columns is 10 × 10 × 10 or 1,000.
• Multiply the number of hectometers by 1,000. 5 × 1,000 = 5,000

           5 hm = 5,000 dm

• Divide to convert smaller units to larger units.

Example   14 dL = _____ kL

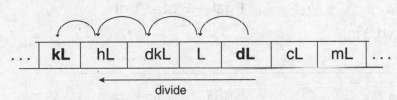

| ... | **kL** | hL | dkL | L | **dL** | cL | mL | ... |

divide

• Find **deci**liters column in the chart. **Kilo**liters are four columns to the left. Each column represents a power of 10; 4 columns is 10 × 10 × 10 × 10 or 10,000.
• Divide the number of deciliters by 10,000. 14 ÷ 10,000 = 0.0014

Remember that in the metric system, units are always expressed as decimals.

           14 dL = 0.0014 kL

PRACTICE

Convert each measurement to the unit indicated.

1. 500 g = _____ mg

2. 1 km = _____ cm

3. 2,000 mL = _____ L

4. 25 cg = _____ mg

5. 37 dL = _____ L

6. 125 hm = _____ m

7. 10 mL = _____ L

8. 4 kg = _____ dkg

9. 30 cm = _____ m

10. 250 dkg = _____ g

Adding and Subtracting Units of Measure

You will often need to convert units to regroup before you can add or subtract. You may also need to convert units to simplify an answer.

When working in the metric system, use the basic conversion rates based on tens.

Example   Subtract 37 cm from 5 m.

$$
\begin{array}{r}
5\text{ m} \\
-37\text{ cm} \\
\hline
\end{array}
$$

Think: 1 m = 100 cm

$$
\begin{array}{r}
\overset{4}{\cancel{5}}\text{ m }100\text{ cm} \\
-37\text{ cm} \\
\hline
4\text{ m }63\text{ cm}
\end{array}
$$

When working in the customary system, be sure to check the conversion rates. They are different for each type of measurement.

Examples   Add 2 ft 8 in. + 3 ft 7 in.

$$
\begin{array}{r}
2\text{ ft }8\text{ in.} \\
+\;3\text{ ft }7\text{ in.} \\
\hline
5\text{ ft }15\text{ in.}
\end{array}
$$

Think: 12 in. = 1 ft   5 ft 15 in. = 6 ft 3 in.

Think: 3 ft = 1 yd 6 ft 3 in. = 2 yd 3 in.
       6 ft = 2 yd

2 ft 8 in. + 3 ft 7 in. = 2 yd 3 in.

Subtract 1 gal − 3 qts.

$$
\begin{array}{r}
1\text{ gal} \\
-\;3\text{ qt} \\
\hline
\end{array}
$$

Think: 1 gal = 4 qt

$$
\begin{array}{r}
\overset{0}{\cancel{1\text{ gal}}}\;4\text{ qt} \\
-3\text{ qt} \\
\hline
1\text{ qt}
\end{array}
$$

1 gal − 3 qt = 1 qt

PRACTICE

Add. Convert to greater units in the answer when possible.

1.
$$
\begin{array}{r}
4\text{ ft }8\text{ in.} \\
+\;1\text{ ft }6\text{ in.} \\
\hline
\end{array}
$$

2.
$$
\begin{array}{r}
2\text{ yd }1\text{ ft} \\
+4\text{ ft} \\
\hline
\end{array}
$$

3.
$$
\begin{array}{r}
1\text{ lb }9\text{ oz} \\
+8\text{ oz} \\
\hline
\end{array}
$$

4.
$$
\begin{array}{r}
3\text{ qt }1\text{ c} \\
+3\text{ c} \\
\hline
\end{array}
$$

5.
$$
\begin{array}{r}
350\text{ mL} \\
+\;875\text{ mL} \\
\hline
\end{array}
$$

6.
$$
\begin{array}{r}
2\text{ ft }6\text{ in.} \\
+9\text{ in.} \\
\hline
\end{array}
$$

7.
$$
\begin{array}{r}
4\text{ fl oz} \\
+\;7\text{ fl oz} \\
\hline
\end{array}
$$

Subtract.

8.
$$
\begin{array}{r}
5\text{ ft }8\text{ in.} \\
-\;1\text{ ft }10\text{ in.} \\
\hline
\end{array}
$$

9.
$$
\begin{array}{r}
3\text{ yd }2\text{ ft} \\
-1\text{ ft }5\text{ in.} \\
\hline
\end{array}
$$

10.
$$
\begin{array}{r}
22\text{ cg} \\
-35\text{ mg} \\
\hline
\end{array}
$$

11.
$$
\begin{array}{r}
1\text{ lb }2\text{ oz} \\
-7\text{ oz} \\
\hline
\end{array}
$$

12.
$$
\begin{array}{r}
2\text{ qt} \\
-1\text{ pt} \\
\hline
\end{array}
$$

13.
$$
\begin{array}{r}
3\text{ km} \\
-150\text{ m} \\
\hline
\end{array}
$$

14.
$$
\begin{array}{r}
1\text{ yr} \\
-5\text{ mo} \\
\hline
\end{array}
$$

15.
$$
\begin{array}{r}
1\text{ T} \\
-550\text{ lb} \\
\hline
\end{array}
$$

Reading a Scale

A number line on a measurement tool such as a ruler or thermometer is called a **scale**. The line is divided equally into units that are marked with numbers. Often, the spaces between the units are divided into fractional units with small lines called **tick marks**.

To find the value represented by tick marks, count the number of spaces created between each pair of numbers on the scale. The numbers on the number line above are 1 unit apart. The longer tick marks between the numbers divide the space into two equal parts, so the longer mark represents $\frac{1}{2}$ of a unit. The spaces are also divided into four equal parts with shorter tick marks that represent $\frac{1}{4}$ of a unit. Note that the $\frac{1}{2}$ mark is also the $\frac{2}{4}$ mark.

PRACTICE

For Questions 1–4, circle the value of the unit represented by each tick mark between the numbers.

1.

   A $\frac{1}{4}$ C $\frac{1}{6}$

   B $\frac{1}{8}$ D $\frac{1}{10}$

2.

   F $\frac{1}{8}$ H $\frac{1}{10}$

   G $\frac{1}{12}$ J $\frac{1}{16}$

3.

   A $\frac{1}{10}$ C $\frac{1}{12}$

   B $\frac{1}{16}$ D $\frac{1}{20}$

4.

   F $\frac{1}{6}$ H $\frac{1}{3}$

   G $\frac{1}{2}$ J $\frac{1}{4}$

Circle the value represented by the pointer.

5.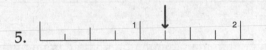

   A 1

   B $1\frac{1}{4}$

   C $1\frac{1}{2}$

   D $1\frac{2}{3}$

6.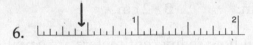

   F $\frac{1}{2}$

   G $\frac{5}{8}$

   H $\frac{3}{4}$

   J $\frac{7}{16}$

Using a Ruler

Rulers, meter sticks, yardsticks, and tape measures use scales to measure length.

Inches are used in the customary system. The space between each inch (in.) may be divided into halves, fourths, eighths, or sixteenths. The longest tick marks will be for inches; $\frac{1}{2}$-inch marks are a little shorter, $\frac{1}{4}$-inch marks shorter still, and so on. The inch ruler below has marks that represent inch, $\frac{1}{2}$-inch, and $\frac{1}{4}$-inch units.

Metric rulers use centimeters. The space between each centimeter (cm) is divided into 10 equal spaces. The tick marks between centimeters represents millimeters (mm).

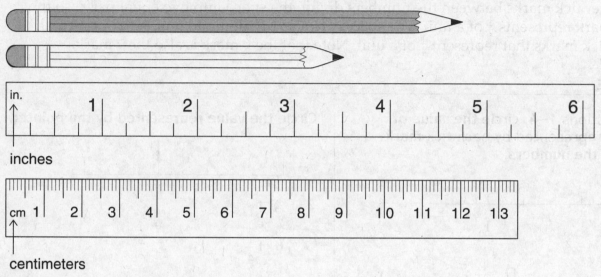

PRACTICE

Use the rulers above to answer each of the following questions.

1. Which represents the greater length?
   A 1 in.   B 2 cm

2. About how many centimeters are equal to 1 inch?
   F 2   G $2\frac{1}{2}$

3. What is the smallest unit of measure shown on the inch ruler above?
   A $\frac{1}{8}$ in.   C $\frac{1}{4}$ in.
   B $\frac{1}{2}$ in.   D 1 in.

4. What is the length of the longer pencil?
   F $3\frac{3}{4}$ in.   H $4\frac{1}{4}$ in.
   G $4\frac{2}{4}$ in.   J $4\frac{3}{4}$ in.

5. What is the length of the shorter pencil?
   A $3\frac{1}{2}$ cm   C $4\frac{3}{4}$ cm
   B 9 cm   D 12 cm

6. Which best describes the difference in length between the two pencils?
   F between $\frac{1}{4}$ inch and $\frac{1}{2}$ inch
   G between $\frac{1}{2}$ inch and 1 inch
   H between 1 inch and $1\frac{1}{2}$ inches
   J between $1\frac{1}{2}$ inches and 2 inches

Reading a Scale That Skips Numbers

Sometimes a scale skips numbers. For example, thermometers and bathroom scales are usually labeled in tens: 10, 20, 30, 40, and so on. On such scales, the tick marks represent whole numbers, not fractions. Follow these steps to figure out what the tick marks represent.

- Find the difference between two neighboring numbers on the scale.
- Count the number of spaces between the two numbers.
- Divide the difference between the numbers by the number of spaces.

Example   Find the reading on this scale.

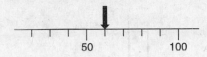

The difference between 50 and 100 is 50.
There are 5 spaces between the numbers.
50 ÷ 5 = 10. Each tick mark represents 10 units.

The reading on the scale is 50 + 10, or 60 units.

Sometimes you can use judgement to read the scale.

Example   Find the reading on this scale.

The pointer on the scale is about halfway between 10 and 20.
15 is halfway between 10 and 20.

The reading on this scale is about 15.

PRACTICE

Identify the value represented by each tick mark for Questions 1–4.

1.
   The space between 10 and 20 is divided into 5 equal spaces.
   Each tick mark represents _____

2.
   The space between 20 and 40 is divided into 10 equal spaces.
   Each tick mark represents _____

3. The space between 60 and 80 is divided into 5 equal spaces.
   Each tick mark represents _____

4. The space between 0 and 50 is divided into 5 equal spaces.
   Each tick mark represents _____

Give the reading described.

5. The pointer is halfway between 20 and 30. _____

6. The pointer is halfway between 50 and 100. _____

7. The pointer is $\frac{1}{4}$ of the way between 0 and 20. _____

8. The pointer is $\frac{3}{4}$ of the way between 0 and 20. _____

9.
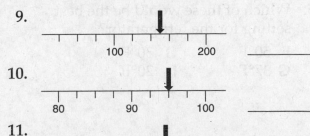
_____

10.

_____

11.
_____

Measuring Temperature

A **thermometer** uses a scale to measure temperature. In the customary system, temperature is measured in **degrees Fahrenheit** (°F). The metric system uses **degrees Celsius** (°C). Look for one of those two symbols on a thermometer to tell you which units are used.

PRACTICE

Use this thermometer for Questions 1–4.

1. Circle the unit this thermometer uses

   degrees Celsius

   degrees Fahrenheit

2. What temperature is shown on the thermometer? _____

3. Is 20°F colder or warmer than the temperature shown above? _____

4. Water freezes at the temperature shown above. Which of these would be the best setting for your freezer?

   A 45°F   C 56°F
   B 37°F   D 5°F

5. Which of these would be the best setting for the refrigerator?

   F 50°F   H 30°F
   G 37°F   J 20°F

This thermometer shows both degrees Celsius and degrees Fahrenheit. Use it for Questions 6–9.

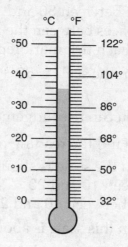

6. Circle the unit that is larger.

   1°C   1°F

7. How many degrees does each tick mark on the above scales represent?

   _____ °C   _____ °F

8. What temperature is shown on the thermometer?

   about _____ °C   about _____ °F

9. Which of these represents the hottest temperature?

   A 104°F   C 40°C
   B 50°C   D 86°F

Finding Perimeter

Perimeter is the distance around the outside of a closed figure. To find the perimeter, add the lengths of the sides to find the total. The letter P is used to represent perimeter.

Examples

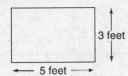

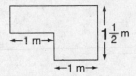

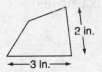

- Find the length of each side. Opposite sides of a rectangle are equal.

  bottom = 5 ft   top = 5 ft

  right side = 3 ft   left side = 3 ft

- Add.

  $P = 5 + 5 + 3 + 3 = 16$

  $P = 16$ ft

- Find the length of each side.

  2 "bottoms" = 2 m   top = 2 m

  right side = $1\frac{1}{2}$ m   2 left sides = $1\frac{1}{2}$ m

- Add.

  $P = 2 + 2 + 1\frac{1}{2} + 1\frac{1}{2} = 7$ m

  $P = 7$ m

There is not enough information to calculate the perimeter of this figure.

PRACTICE

Find the perimeter of each shape. *Hint:* The symbol " is an abbreviation for inches and the symbol ' is an abbreviation for feet.

1. a rectangular room 12 feet long and 5 feet wide

   $P = $ _____

2.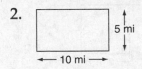

   $P = $ _____

3.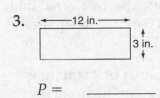

   $P = $ _____

4.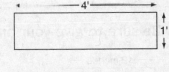

   $P = $ _____

5. a square that measures 2 cm on each side

   $P = $ _____

6.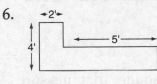

   $P = $ _____

7.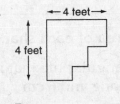

   $P = $ _____

8. The perimeter of a rectangle is 20 cm. The top and bottom are each 8 cm long. What is the length of each side of the rectangle?

   _____

Finding Area

Area is the size of a surface and is usually measured in square units such as square feet (ft²), square yards (yd²), square meters (m²), and so on. One way to find area is to count the number of squares inside a shape. The letter A is used to represent area.

Examples

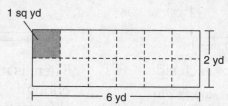

This rectangle is divided into squares that measure 1 yard on each side. Each small square is 1 sq yd, or 1 yd².
$A = 12$ yd²

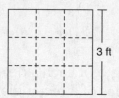

Each side of the square is divided into foot-long sections to create 9 smaller squares inside the shape. Each smaller square is 1 sq ft, or 1 ft².
$A = 9$ ft²

A shortcut to finding the area of a square or a rectangle is to multiply *length* × *width*. However, the length and width must be the same unit of measure.

• For the rectangle on the left, $A = l \times w = 2$ yd $\times$ 6 yd $= 12$ yd².

• For the square on the right, $A = l \times w = 3$ ft $\times$ 3 ft $= 9$ ft².

PRACTICE

Find the area of each shape below. Be sure to give your answers in square units.

1. a rectangular tile that is 6 cm long and 6 cm wide

   $A =$ _____

2. a rectangle whose sides measure 2 mm, 4 mm, 2 mm, and 4 mm

   $A =$ _____

3.
   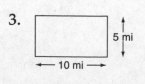

   $A =$ _____

4. 12 inches, 3 inches

   $A =$ _____

5. 4 ft, 1 ft

   $A =$ _____

6. a square that measures 2 cm on each side

   $A =$ _____

7. 3 m, 3 m

   $A =$ _____

   (*Hint:* The area is *not* that of a 6 m × 6 m square.)

8. The area of a square is 25 square inches. How long is each side of the square?

   _____

Reading Time

We use clocks and watches to measure units of time such as seconds, minutes, and hours. Digital clocks (Figure A) show hours separated from minutes with a colon. Analog clocks (Figure B) have hands that move around a face. It is important to be able to read both types of clocks.

Figure A   Figure B

- With a digital clock, read the number left of the colon (:) as the hour, and the number at the right of the colon as minutes. The digital clock above would be read 4:43 (four forty-three), which means 43 minutes *after* 4 o'clock, or 43 minutes *past* 4 o'clock.

- With an analog clock, you can read the time as minutes after the last hour, or as minutes before the next hour. The clock in Figure B can be read as 4:43. It can also be read as 17 minutes *before* 5, or 17 minutes *to* 5. Notice that 43 minutes (after) + 17 minutes (before) = 60 minutes or 1 hour.

$$15 \text{ minutes} = \tfrac{1}{4} \text{ hour or a quarter of an hour}$$

$$30 \text{ minutes} = \tfrac{1}{2} \text{ hour or half of an hour}$$

$$45 \text{ minutes} = \tfrac{3}{4} \text{ hour or 3 quarters of an hour}$$

PRACTICE

Circle the correct answer.

1. What time is shown on the clock? There are two correct answers.

   A 4:30
   B half past five
   C half past four
   D 5:30

2. What time is shown on the clock? There are two correct answers.

   F 20 minutes to 9
   G 8 minutes to 9
   H 8 minutes past 8
   J 8:40

3. What time will the clock show in 15 minutes?

   A 2:15
   B 2:20
   C 2:25
   D 3:30

4. What time will the clock show in 30 minutes?

   F 15 minutes to 3
   G 25 minutes before 3
   H 35 minutes before 3
   J 35 minutes after 3

Fill in the blank to convert each amount of time shown.

5. $\tfrac{1}{2}$ hour = _____ min

6. 2 hours = _____ min

7. $\tfrac{1}{3}$ hour = _____ min

8. 2 days = _____ hr

9. $1\tfrac{1}{2}$ hours = _____ min

10. $\tfrac{3}{4}$ hour = _____ min

Calculating Time

When you know how long a task will take, you can figure out what time to start the task in order to finish by a certain time. You can also figure out what time you will finish the task if you start it at a certain time. You can use a clock face to help with that.

Examples

You have an appointment at 10:00. It takes 1 hour and 15 minutes to travel. What time should you start out?

Since you need a time *before* 10:00, count back from 10:00.
- Count the hours. Start at 10:00. 1 hour before 10:00 is 9:00.
- Count the minutes. Start at 9:00. 15 minutes before 9:00 is 8:45.

You should start out at 8:45.

Eric starts work at 8:45. He works for 7 hours and 45 minutes. What time does he finish work?

Since the time will be *after* 8:45, count forward.
- Count the hours. Start at 8:45. 7 hours after 8:45 is 3:45.
- Count the minutes. Start at 3:45. 45 minutes after 3:45 is 4:30.

Eric finishes work at 4:30.

PRACTICE

Write the time asked for in each problem.

1. What is the time exactly 5 hours before 2:00?

   _____

2. What is the time exactly 6 hours after 9:00?

   _____

3. It will take 6 hours to make bread. You plan to eat at 5:00. By what time should you start making the bread?

   _____

4. It will take 50 minutes to drive to your mother's house. You leave at 3:30. When will you arrive?

   _____

5. Gregory volunteers at a shelter. He spent $5\frac{1}{2}$ hours there on Tuesday. If he started at 8:15 A.M., what time did he leave?

   _____

6. When Sabrina checked her watch, it was 3:30. She had been reading for 1 hour and 45 minutes. What time did she start reading?

   _____

Finding Elapsed Time

The amount of time that passes between the beginning of a task or event and its end is called **elapsed time**. To find elapsed time, find the difference between the starting time and the ending time. You can use a clock face to help you find elapsed time. Keep in mind that 12:00 midnight starts the A.M. or morning hours; 12:00 noon starts the P.M. or afternoon hours.

Examples

Sheeri's train is scheduled to leave the station at 9:45 A.M. The train should arrive at her stop at 1:30 P.M. How long will Sheeri be on the train?

- Count the hours.
  Start at 9:45. Count complete hours.
  From 9:45 to 12:45 is 3 hours.
- Count the minutes.
  Start at 12:45. Count the number of minutes until 1:30.
  From 12:45 to 1:30 is 45 minutes.

Sheeri will be on the train for 3 hours and 45 minutes.

Note: Another way to find the answer would be to count the hours from 9:45 to 1:45, and then subtract the number of minutes as you count back from 1:45 to 1:30.

PRACTICE

Find the elapsed time for each situation.

1. Start time: 6:20 A.M.
   Stop time: 11:25 A.M.
   Elapsed time: _____

2. Start time: 10:30 A.M.
   Stop time: 2:15 P.M.
   Elapsed time: _____

3. The decorating committee began putting up decorations for the party at 3:20 P.M. It was 7:45 P.M. when they finished. How long did it take the committee to finish the job? _____

4. Renaldo and Carl finished painting the bedroom at 3:20 P.M. They had started painting at 9:15 that morning. How long did it take them to paint the bedroom? _____

5. Gretchen said she would meet Falon at 2:15 that afternoon, but she got stuck in traffic and didn't show up until 3:05. How late was Gretchen? _____

6. Warren started typing his report at 8:30 A.M. and didn't finish until 2:50 that afternoon. How long did it take him to finish the report? _____

Adding and Subtracting Time

When you add or subtract amounts of time, you need to add or subtract like units. You may need to convert units. Remember, 60 minutes = 1 hour.

Examples

$$
\begin{array}{ll}
& 1 \text{ hour} \quad 15 \text{ minutes} \\
+ & 2 \text{ hours} \quad 50 \text{ minutes} \\
\hline
& 3 \text{ hours} \quad 65 \text{ minutes}
\end{array}
$$

$$
\begin{array}{ll}
& \overset{2}{\cancel{3}} \text{ hours} \quad \overset{70}{\cancel{10}} \text{ minutes} \\
- & \phantom{3 \text{ hours} \quad} 45 \text{ minutes} \\
\hline
& 2 \text{ hours} \quad 25 \text{ minutes}
\end{array}
$$

Simplify the answer.
• Convert 60 minutes to 1 hour.
  65 min = 1 hr 5 min
• Add.
  3 hr + 1 hr + 5 min

  3 hr 65 min = 4 hr 5 min

Regroup to subtract.
• Convert 1 hour to 60 minutes.
• Add. 60 min + 10 min = 70 min
• Subtract.

PRACTICE

Add or subtract. Regroup to convert minutes to hours or hours to minutes as needed.

1. $\begin{array}{l} 1 \text{ hour} \quad 15 \text{ minutes} \\ + 4 \text{ hours} \quad 30 \text{ minutes} \\ \hline \end{array}$

6. $\begin{array}{l} 4 \text{ hours} \\ - 1 \text{ hour} \quad 25 \text{ minutes} \\ \hline \end{array}$

2. $\begin{array}{l} 45 \text{ minutes} \\ + 45 \text{ minutes} \\ \hline \end{array}$

7. $\begin{array}{l} 5 \text{ hours} \quad 10 \text{ minutes} \\ - 2 \text{ hours} \quad 20 \text{ minutes} \\ \hline \end{array}$

3. $\begin{array}{l} 3 \text{ hours} \quad 35 \text{ minutes} \\ + 2 \text{ hours} \quad 45 \text{ minutes} \\ \hline \end{array}$

8. $\begin{array}{l} 6 \text{ hours} \quad 15 \text{ minutes} \\ - 3 \text{ hours} \quad 40 \text{ minutes} \\ \hline \end{array}$

4. $\begin{array}{l} 5 \text{ hours} \quad 10 \text{ minutes} \\ + 3 \text{ hours} \quad 50 \text{ minutes} \\ \hline \end{array}$

9. $\begin{array}{l} 1 \text{ hour} \quad 30 \text{ minutes} \\ - \phantom{1 \text{ hour} \quad} 45 \text{ minutes} \\ \hline \end{array}$

5. $\begin{array}{l} 1 \text{ hour} \quad 15 \text{ minutes} \\ + 3 \text{ hours} \quad 39 \text{ minutes} \\ \phantom{+ 3 \text{ hours} \quad} 30 \text{ minutes} \\ \hline \end{array}$

10. $\begin{array}{l} 4 \text{ hours} \quad 12 \text{ minutes} \\ - 2 \text{ hours} \quad 27 \text{ minutes} \\ \hline \end{array}$

Measurement Skills Checkup

Circle the letter for the correct answer to each problem.

1. What time will the clock show in 20 minutes?

   A 2:20   C 3:20

   B 2:55   D 3:05

2. A pork chop weighs 8 ounces. What fraction of a pound is that?

   F $\frac{1}{4}$ H $\frac{1}{2}$

   G $\frac{1}{3}$ J $\frac{1}{5}$

3. Which is the most reasonable estimate of the height of a door?

   A   7 inches

   B   70 inches

   C   700 inches

   D 7,000 inches

4. You want to make a $\frac{1}{4}$-pound hamburger. How many ounces of hamburger do you need?

   F 10 oz   H 4 oz

   G 25 oz   J 40 oz

5. Maya leaves her children with the babysitter at 6:50 P.M. She returns at 8:45 P.M. How long are her children with the babysitter?

   A 1 hour and 55 minutes

   B 1 hour and 5 minutes

   C 2 hours and 5 minutes

   D 3 hours and 5 minutes

This diagram shows plans for a picture frame. Study the diagram. Then do Numbers 6–8.

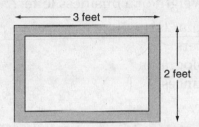

6. What is the perimeter along the outside edge of this picture frame?

   F 5 ft   H 10 ft

   G 6 ft   J 8 ft

7. What is the area of the framed picture?

   A 6 sq ft   C 10 sq ft

   B 5 sq ft   D 8 sq ft

8. It takes about 25 minutes to cut the materials for this frame. It takes another 45 minutes to put them together. How long does it take to make the frame?

   F 1 hour and 10 minutes

   G 1 hour and 7 minutes

   H 1 hour and 20 minutes

   J $1\frac{1}{2}$ hours

9. What temperature is shown on this thermometer?

   A 65°C

   B 63°C

   C $1\frac{1}{2}$°C

   D 66°C

Measurement Skills Checkup (continued)

10. Which unit would be used to measure the weight of a business letter?

    F pounds
    G liters
    H kilograms
    J ounces

11. Byung plans to spend 20 minutes exercising on a stair machine. He starts at 4:52. When will he finish?

    A 5:12   C 5:02
    B 4:72   D 5:07

12. Rochelle buys 20 feet of fence for her garden. She plans to use all 20 feet to outline one square flower bed. How long will each side of the flower bed be?

    F 10 feet   H 4 feet
    G 5 feet   J 3 feet

13. You want to buy 8 ounces of peas. They cost $1.00 per pound. How much will you pay?

    A $1   C $0.50
    B $2   D $0.80

14. Which measure is equal to 1 kL?

    F 1,000 cL   H 1,000 dL
    G 1,000 mL   J 1,000 L

15. Grace has a ribbon that is 3 feet long. She needs to use 32 inches to trim her hem. How much ribbon will she have left over?

    A 10 inches   C 4 inches
    B   8 inches   D 2 inches

16. A train trip from Forest to Central takes 40 minutes. Continuing on the train from Central to the zoo takes another 50 minutes. How long is the ride from Forest all the way to the zoo?

    F 1 hour and 10 minutes
    G 1 hour and 20 minutes
    H 1 hour and 30 minutes
    J 1 hour and 40 minutes

17. Which of these is the best tool for finding out if a refrigerator will fit through a doorway?

    A calendar   C ruler
    B thermometer   D clock

18. Which of the following would be a comfortable temperature for your bath water? (Body temperature ≈ 98° F)

    F 20°F   H 100°F
    G 50°F   J 200°F

19. Here are the dimensions of three rectangular fields.

    Field A: 50 feet by 20 feet
    Field B: 30 feet by 30 feet
    Field C: 30 feet by 40 feet

    Which field has the greatest area?

    A Field A
    B Field B
    C Field C
    D They all have the same area.

20. Which is the most reasonable estimate for the weight of a kitten?

    F 5 oz   H 5 T
    G 5 lb   J 5 g

Geometry

Naming Points, Lines, Line Segments, and Rays

Geometry is the branch of mathematics that deals with lines, points, curves, angles, surfaces, and solids, and with relationships among these things. The chart below contains basic terms used in geometry.

Term	Definition	Symbol
point	a location on an object or a position in space	A point is shown by a capital letter. $\dot{M}$ G $\dot{A}$
line	a connected set of points that extends without end in two directions	Two letters on the line are used to name the line. Line PQ is written $\overleftrightarrow{PQ}$. This line can also be called $\overleftrightarrow{QP}$.
line segment	two points (endpoints) and the straight path between them	endpoints $A \bullet\!\!-\!\!-\!\!-\!\!\bullet B$ A line segment is a section of a line. It is named by its endpoints. Line segment AB is written $\overline{AB}$. This line segment can also be called $\overline{BA}$.
ray	part of a line that extends in one direction	W X Ray WX is written $\overrightarrow{WX}$. The endpoint is always given first.

PRACTICE

Name each figure.

1.  T S

_____

2.  G H

_____

3.  K L

_____

4.  X Y

_____

5. 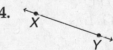 M N

_____

6. 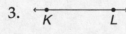 E F

_____

Naming Angles

An **angle** is formed by two rays that share the same endpoint. The endpoint is the **vertex** of the angle, and the two rays form the **sides** of the angle. The symbol for an angle is ∠.

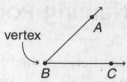

- Angles can be named by their vertex letter, or with three letters. The angle at right is ∠B, or ∠ABC, or ∠CBA. If two or more angles share the same vertex, use three letters; the vertex letter must be the middle letter.

An angle is measured in by the number of degrees between the rays. Think of an angle as part of a circle with its vertex at the center. A circle is 360°.

- A **straight angle** cuts the circle in half. It has 180°.
- A **right angle** is $\frac{1}{4}$ of a circle. It is 90°.

  The symbol for a right angle is a small square in the angle.

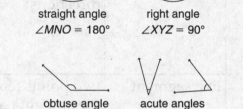

straight angle
∠MNO = 180°

right angle
∠XYZ = 90°

- An acute angle is less than 90°.
- An **obtuse angle** is greater than 90°, but less than 180°.

obtuse angle   acute angles

PRACTICE

Use the drawing below to answer Questions 1–4. Circle the correct answer.

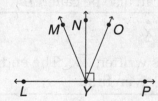

1. Which of these does *not* name an angle in the above drawing?

   A ∠MYN   C ∠YPO
   B ∠NYL   D ∠OYL

2. Which is an obtuse angle?

   F ∠MYP   H ∠MYO
   G ∠OYP   J ∠NYP

3. Which is an acute angle?

   A ∠LYO   C ∠NYP
   B ∠PYM   D ∠LYM

4. Which is a straight angle?

   F ∠OYP   H ∠LYP
   G ∠MYO   J ∠OYL

Circle the letter of the smaller angle in each pair.

5.

A   B

6.

F   G

Investigating Lines

Lines that cross, or that will cross, are called **intersecting lines**. The point at which they cross is called the **point of intersection**.

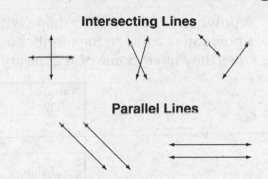

Intersecting Lines

Lines that are always the same distance apart are **parallel lines**. Parallel lines will never intersect. The symbol ∥ means "is parallel to."

Parallel Lines

Lines that form right angles when they intersect are called **perpendicular lines**. The symbol ⊥ means "is perpendicular to."

Perpendicular Lines

PRACTICE

Use the figures below to answer Questions 1–3.

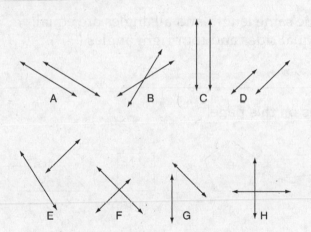

A   B   C   D

E   F   G   H

1. Which letters label pairs
    of lines that intersect?   _____

2. Which letters label pairs
    of lines that are parallel? _____

3. Which letters label pairs
    of perpendicular lines?   _____

Use this map for Questions 4 and 5.

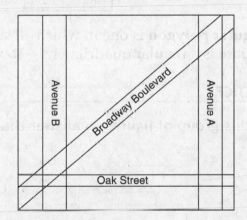

4. Which streets are perpendicular to
    each other?

    _____

    _____

5. Which two streets are parallel?

    _____

    _____

Reviewing Polygons

A **polygon** is a closed flat shape with three or more straight sides. The number of angles in a polygon is equal to the number of sides. Polygons are named according to the number of sides they have. Some polygons are listed below.

Name of Polygon	Example	Number of Sides/Angles
triangle		3
quadrilateral		4
pentagon		5
hexagon		6
octagon		8
decagon		10

A **regular polygon** is one in which all sides are the same length and all angles are equal. A square is a regular quadrilateral—it has four equal sides and four right angles (90°).

PRACTICE

Use this group of figures to answer the questions on this page.

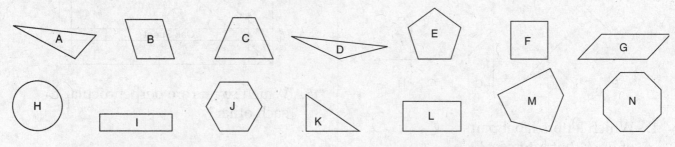

1. Which three figures are triangles?

   _____

2. Which six figures are quadrilaterals?

   _____

3. Which two figures are pentagons?

   _____

4. Which figure is a hexagon?

   _____

5. Which figure is a square?

   _____

6. Which four polygons are regular?

   _____

7. Which figure is *not* a polygon?

   _____

8. Which figure is an octagon?

   _____

Recognizing Special Quadrilaterals

A quadrilateral is a polygon that has four sides and four angles. Within the family of quadrilaterals, figures are further classified according to their sides and angles.

Quadrilateral	Definition	Examples
parallelogram	A quadrilateral whose opposite sides are parallel. Opposite sides and opposite angles are equal.	
rectangle	A parallelogram with 4 right angles. Opposite sides are equal, but all 4 sides do not have to be equal.	
square	A rectangle with 4 equal sides	
rhombus	A parallelogram with 4 equal sides. Opposite angles are equal, but all 4 angles of a rhombus do not have to be equal. A square is a rhombus with 4 equal angles.	
trapezoid	A quadrilateral that has only 1 pair of parallel sides	

PRACTICE

Use this group of figures to answer Questions 1–4.

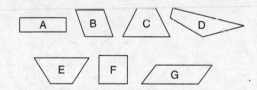

1. Write the letter of each figure that is a parallelogram. _____

2. Write the letter of each figure that is a rectangle. _____

3. Write the letter of each figure that is a trapezoid. _____

4. Write the letter of each figure that is a rhombus. _____

Write *True* or *False*.

5. A square is a parallelogram. _____

6. Some rectangles are squares. _____

7. A trapezoid is *not* a parallelogram. _____

8. All squares are rectangles. _____

9. All rectangles are parallelograms. _____

10. Some rhombuses are squares. _____

Working with Triangles

Here are two important facts about triangles:
- The sum of the three angles for every triangle is 180°.
- The sum of any two sides of a triangle must be greater than the third side.

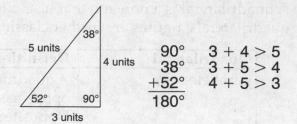

$$
\begin{array}{ll}
90° & 3 + 4 > 5 \\
38° & 3 + 5 > 4 \\
+52° & 4 + 5 > 3 \\
\hline
180° &
\end{array}
$$

- Triangles can be named in two ways.

By lengths of sides:
equilateral—three equal sides*
isosceles—at least two equal sides
scalene—three sides of different lengths

By measures of angles:
acute—each angle measures less than 90°
right—one right angle (90°)
obtuse—one angle measuring greater than 90°

The triangle shown above is both right and scalene.

Note: An equilateral triangle is a regular polygon. It has three equal sides and three equal angles. The marks on each side indicate that the sides are congruent.

PRACTICE

For Questions 1–4, find the measure of the third angle. Then identify each triangle as acute, right, or obtuse.

1.

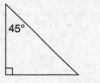

_____

2.

_____

3.

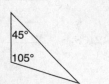

_____

4.

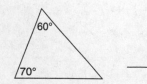

_____

Name each triangle by angle measures and by lengths of sides.

5.

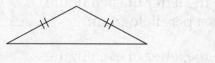

_____

6.

_____

7.

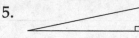

_____

8.

_____

Investigating Circles

A **circle** is the set of all points that are the same distance from a given point called the **center**. When you see a dot at the center of the circle, you can assume it represents the center point of the circle.

- The distance from the center to any point on the circle is the **radius** of the circle.
- A line segment with endpoints that lie on the circle is a **chord**.
- A chord that passes through the center of the circle is called a **diameter**. The diameter is the circle's longest chord. The diameter of a circle is twice as long as its radius.

PRACTICE

Use the figure below to answer Questions 1–4.

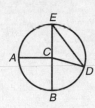

1. Name two radii.

   _____

2. Name two chords.

   _____

3. Name a diameter.

   _____

4. Name a chord that is not a diameter.

   _____

Find the diameter of each circle below. If there is not enough information, write "cannot tell."

5.
2 in.

diameter: _____

6.
3 cm

diameter: _____

7.
3 cm

diameter: _____

Find the radius of each circle below. If there is not enough information, write "cannot tell."

8.
100 mm

radius: _____

9.
4 cm

radius: _____

10.
3 cm

radius: _____

Visualizing Shapes

In geometry, you often have to be able to imagine a figure from a different point of view. You may also need to imagine a shape to draw it.

PRACTICE

Circle the letter of the correct answer to each question.

1. This drawing shows a piece of paper that has been folded in half and then cut as shown. What is the shape of the cutout when it is unfolded?

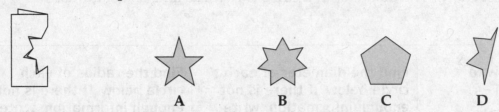

2. What is the shape of this cutout when it is unfolded?

3. If you trace around the bottom of this cylinder, what shape will you draw?

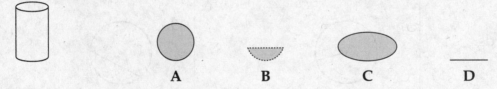

4. If you trace around the bottom of this object, what shape will you draw?

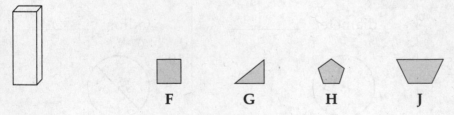

5. If you fold this figure along the dotted line, what is the shape of the *folded* figure?

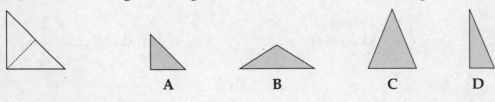

Recognizing Symmetry

If a figure can be divided into two halves that are mirror images of one another, we say the figure has **symmetry**, or is **symmetric**. The line that separates the two halves is called the **line of symmetry**. A shape can have more than one line of symmetry.

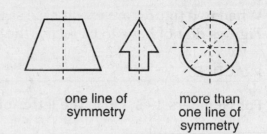

one line of symmetry

more than one line of symmetry

PRACTICE

Circle the letter of the figure in each row that has been divided in half symmetrically.

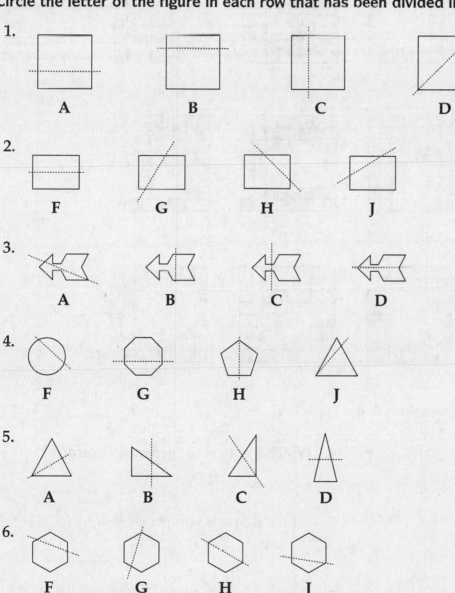

1.
   A   B   C   D

2.
   F   G   H   J

3.
   A   B   C   D

4.
   F   G   H   J

5.
   A   B   C   D

6.
   F   G   H   J

Circle each letter below that can be divided in half symmetrically.

7. A M G Y   8. F J H X

Recognizing Congruent Figures

When two figures are exactly the same size and shape, they are **congruent**.
Figures do not have to be facing the same direction to be congruent.

PRACTICE

For Numbers 1–3, circle the letter of the figure that is congruent to the one in the dark box.

1.

A   B   C

2.

F   G   H

3.

A   B   C

Use the diagram below for Questions 4–6.

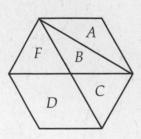

4. Which figure is congruent to figure *A*?

   _____

5. Which figure is congruent to figure *C*?

   _____

6. Which 2 figures joined together form a shape that is congruent to figure *D*?

   _____

Recognizing Similar Figures

When two figures have exactly the same shape, but not necessarily the same size, they are **similar**. Figures do not have to be facing the same direction to be similar.

PRACTICE

For Questions 1–3, circle the letter of the shape that appears to be similar to the shaded figure.

1.

    A   B   C   D

2.

    F   G   H   J

3.

    A   B   C   D

Use the diagram below to answer Questions 4 and 5.

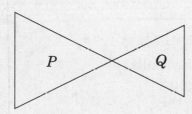

4. Do triangles P and Q look similar?

    _____

5. Do triangles P and Q look congruent?

    _____

Use the diagram below to answer Questions 6 and 7.

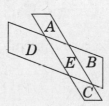

6. Which figure, if any, looks similar to figure A?

    _____

7. Which figure, if any, looks similar to figure B?

    _____

Comparing Three-Dimensional Figures

A **three-dimensional figure** has length, width, and depth. Three-dimensional figures are also called **solid figures**. A flat surface of a three-dimensional solid is called a **face**.

Some common three-dimensional figures are described here.

- A **rectangular solid** is the shape of a box. It has 6 faces, and each face is a rectangle. Every corner of a rectangular solid forms a right angle.

- A **cube** is a rectangular solid with 6 square faces. Every corner of a cube forms a right angle.

- A **cylinder** is shaped like a can. The top and bottom surfaces are circles.

- A **cone** has one circular face. At the opposite end, the cone comes to a point.

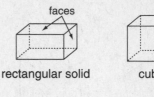
rectangular solid   cube

cylinder   cone

PRACTICE

Identify which shape each of the following objects looks most like. Write cube, rectangular solid, cylinder, or cone.

1. a shoebox _____

2. a roll of paper towels _____

3. each of a pair of dice _____

4. a Christmas tree _____

5. a can of frozen orange juice _____

6. a telephone book _____

7. a drinking glass _____

Use what you know about polygons and solids to answer the questions below.

8. What is the total area of all six faces of this cube? 2"

_____

9. Is this figure a rectangular solid?

_____

10. Which would hold more water, this cylinder or this cone?

_____

Using Geometry in Solving Problems

The problems on this page are different from usual math problems. They can be fun to solve, but they require that you read the question carefully and analyze the information. You can use the problem solving steps to answer these types of questions.

- • **Identify the question.**
- • **Determine what information you need.**
- • **Make a plan.**
- • **Solve the problem.**
- • **Check your work.**

PRACTICE

Write the letter or number that answers the question.

1. Which number is inside the rectangle but outside the triangle?

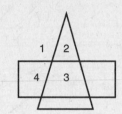

_____

2. Which letter is inside the circle and the square, but outside the triangle?

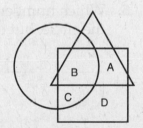

_____

3. Which letter is inside both the obtuse triangle and the acute triangle?

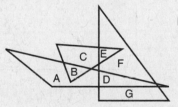

_____

4. Which number is inside only a figure that is not a polygon?

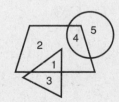

_____

Use the figure below to answer Questions 5–8.

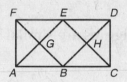

5. Which is an obtuse angle?

    A ∠FAB   **C** ∠BDC
    B ∠FEC   **D** ∠ECB

6. Which is a right angle?

    F ∠ABF   **H** ∠EDC
    G ∠ABG   **J** ∠FEG

7. Which triangle is congruent to △ AEC?

    A △ EDH   **C** △ AGB
    B △ FAB   **D** △ FBD

8. Which figure is *not* a parallelogram?

    F figure FECB
    G figure DCAF
    H figure EGBH
    J figure ACDE

Geometry Skills Checkup

Circle the letter for the best answer to each question.

1. Which sections of this figure are congruent?

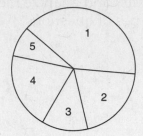

   A 1 and 5
   B 2 and 4
   C 2 and 5
   D 1 and 4

2. Which figures are similar?

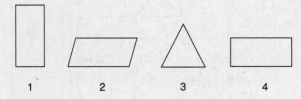

   F 1 and 3
   G 1 and 4
   H 2 and 3
   J 1, 2, and 4

3. What is the measure of angle *A*?

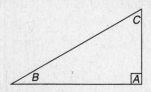

   A   30 degrees
   B   45 degrees
   C   90 degrees
   D 180 degrees

4. Which diagram shows parallel lines?

   F

   G

   H

   J

5. Which number is inside the square and the circle, but outside the triangle?

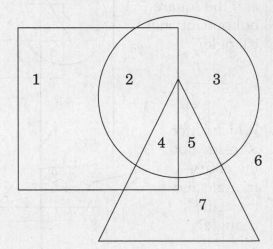

   A 2
   B 4
   C 3
   D 5

6. Which best describes $\overline{AC}$?

    F chord
    G radius
    H diameter
    J line

7. Which best describes this figure?

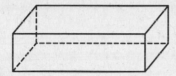

    A cube
    B cone
    C rectangular solid
    D pyramid

8. Which best describes triangle *ABC*?

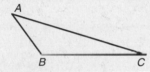

    F acute and scalene
    G obtuse and isosceles
    H right and isosceles
    J obtuse and scalene

9. Which describes the features of a regular polygon?

    A equal sides but not equal angles
    B equal angles but not equal sides
    C neither equal sides nor equal angles
    D both equal sides and equal angles

Use the drawing below to answer Questions 10–12. Circle the term that best describes the relationship between the lines named.

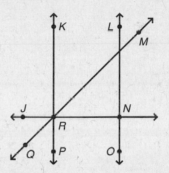

10. $\overleftrightarrow{QM}$ and $\overleftrightarrow{JN}$

    F intersecting
    G parallel
    H similar
    J perpendicular

11. $\overleftrightarrow{KP}$ and $\overleftrightarrow{JN}$

    A intersecting
    B parallel
    C similar
    D perpendicular

12. $\overleftrightarrow{KP}$ and $\overleftrightarrow{LO}$

    F intersecting
    G parallel
    H similar
    J perpendicular

Skills Inventory Posttest

Part A: Computation

Circle the letter of the correct answer to each problem.

1.
$$4 + 5 + 3 =$$
A 13 C 9
B 12 D 11
E None of these

2.
$$461 + 38 =$$
F 841 H 499
G 741 J 489
K None of these

3.
$$\begin{array}{r} 579 \\ -\ 174 \end{array}$$
A 415 C 475
B 403 D 406
E None of these

4.
$$852 + 9 =$$
F 851 H 942
G 861 J 1,752
K None of these

5.
$$21 \times 34 =$$
A 614 C 704
B 147 D 714
E None of these

6.
$$16 \times 10 =$$
F 26 H 160
G 116 J 106
K None of these

7.
$$5\overline{)2,055}$$
A 411 C 511
B 4,011 D 1,511
E None of these

8.
$$6,714 + 27 =$$
F 6,984 H 6,731
G 6,744 J 6,741
K None of these

9.
$$6\overline{)30}$$
A 6 C 4
B 5 D 24
E None of these

10.
$$\begin{array}{r} 2,345 \\ -\ 165 \end{array}$$
F 2,180 H 2,170
G 2,280 J 2,270
K None of these

11.
$$42.5 + 8.37 =$$
A 50.87 C 12.62
B 1.262 D 40.87
E None of these

12.
$$\frac{2}{5} + \frac{3}{10} =$$
F $\frac{5}{15}$ H 1
G $\frac{5}{10}$ J $1\frac{1}{5}$
K None of these

13.
$$\begin{array}{r} 302 \\ -\ 60 \end{array}$$
A 232 C 342
B 242 D 332
E None of these

14.
$$3,125 - 127 =$$
F 3,002 H 2,998
G 3,008 J 3,018
K None of these

15.

$113 \times 27 =$

A 3,051
B 2,051
C 3,017
D 3,031
E None of these

16.

$8 \div 5 =$

F 1
G 2
H 1 R3
J 1 R2
K None of these

17.

$0.3 \times 9 =$

A 27
B 2.7
C 0.27
D 0.027
E None of these

18.

$\dfrac{3}{5} + \dfrac{1}{5} =$

F $\dfrac{2}{5}$ H $\dfrac{4}{25}$

G $\dfrac{4}{5}$ J $\dfrac{3}{5}$

K None of these

19.

$\begin{array}{r} 3,529 \\ + 1,874 \\ \hline \end{array}$

A 5,403
B 4,393
C 5,314
D 5,304
E None of these

20.

$\begin{array}{r} 0.2 \\ \times \quad 0.4 \\ \hline \end{array}$

F 8
G 0.8
H 0.08
J 0.008
K None of these

21.

$\begin{array}{r} \dfrac{4}{5} \\ - \dfrac{2}{5} \\ \hline \end{array}$

A 2
B $\dfrac{2}{5}$
C $\dfrac{2}{10}$
D $\dfrac{2}{25}$
E None of these

22.

$23\overline{)85}$

F 3 R10
G 41 R2
H 12
J 3 R16
K None of these

23.

$\begin{array}{r} 1,245 \\ \times \quad 4 \\ \hline \end{array}$

A 4,840
B 4,960
C 4,860
D 4,880
E None of these

24.

$\begin{array}{r} 12.3 \\ - \quad 0.25 \\ \hline \end{array}$

F 12.5
G 12.15
H 12.05
J 9.8
K None of these

25.

$17 - 1.245 =$

A 15.755
B 16.245
C 16.845
D 15.655
E None of these

Part B: Applied Mathematics

Circle the letter of the correct answer to each question.

1. What number is missing from this number pattern?

    43, 39, 35, 31, 27, 23, ___ , 15, 11

    A 22
    B 25
    C 19
    D 17

2. Which group of numbers is missing from this number pattern?

    3, 6, 9, 12, ___, ___, ___, 24, 27, 30

    F 14, 17, 20
    G 15, 18, 21
    H 15, 19, 22
    J 16, 18, 21

3. Which of these is the same as the number in the place-value chart?

thousands	hundreds	tens	ones
4	3	0	1

    A 431
    B four thousand, thirty-one hundred
    C 4,000 + 300 + 10
    D four thousand, three hundred one

4. Which of these numbers is a common factor of 24 and 32?

    F 6
    G 3
    H 8
    J 12

5. If $5 \times n = 45$, which is the value of n?

    A 8   C 9
    B 5   D 6

6. Erica has 45 pieces of costume jewelry. Each drawer of her jewelry box can hold 12 pieces. How many drawers can she completely fill?

    F 1   H 3
    G 2   J 4

7. Kendall works three days a week at a fast-food restaurant. Last week he served 65 people on Monday, 42 people on Tuesday, and 89 people on Thursday. To estimate how many people he served in all, what numbers should Kendall add?

    A 60, 40, and 80
    B 60, 40, and 90
    C 70, 40, and 90
    D 60, 40, and 100

8. What number goes in the boxes to make both number sentences true?

    $19 - 5 = \square$
    $19 - \square = 5$

    F 12   H 13
    G 14   J 15

9. You earn an extra hour of vacation for every 5 hours of overtime you work. If you work 15 hours of overtime, how many hours of extra vacation time will you get?

    A 3   C 4
    B 5   D 10

This circle graph shows how Ramona spends her time on a typical weekday. Use the graph to answer Numbers 10–13.

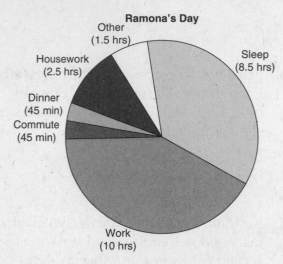

Ramona's Day

Other (1.5 hrs)
Housework (2.5 hrs)
Dinner (45 min)
Commute (45 min)
Sleep (8.5 hrs)
Work (10 hrs)

10. Which activity takes up the least amount of Ramona's time each day?

F work
G dinner
H housework
J other

11. During a 5-day workweek, how much time does Ramona spend commuting?

A 1 hour
B 7 hours
C 3 hours, 45 minutes
D 10 hours

12. On which activity does Ramona spend $\frac{1}{4}$ the amount of time she spends working?

F sleeping
G commuting
H making dinner
J doing housework

13. Yesterday, Ramona spent 2 hours more at work than usual. How many hours did she work yesterday?

A 10 hours
B 8 hours
C 6 hours
D 12 hours

The information below shows how much a particular company charges for walking tours in New York City. Study the chart. Then do Numbers 14–17.

Tour Rates (per person)

$2\frac{1}{2}$ hours in Brooklyn	$13
$3\frac{1}{2}$ hours in Central Park	$10
$2\frac{1}{2}$ hours in Coney Island	$14

14. Joy and her sister each bought a ticket for the tours of Brooklyn and Central Park. How much did their tickets cost?

F $48
G $56
H $46
J $54

15. If the number sentence $L + \$13 = \$22.50$ represents the cost of a tour of Brooklyn plus lunch, what is the cost for the lunch?

A $ 9.50
B $12.50
C $11.50
D $10.50

16. Which is closest to the exact cost to take 5 people on the $2\frac{1}{2}$ hour tour of Coney Island?

F $55
G $60
H $65
J $75

17. Hank buys 2 tickets for the Coney Island tour. He pays with a $50 bill. Which combination of bills represents the correct amount for his change?

A 3 tens
B 2 tens, 4 ones
C 3 fives, 7 ones
D 1 ten, 1 five, 4 ones

Miranda is making a green and white quilt that will have 24 squares. The design for the quilt shown here is incomplete. Study the diagram. Then do Numbers 18–20.

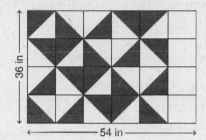

36 in

◄——— 54 in ———►

18. Which design shows how the last column of the quilt should look?

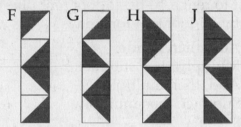

F   G   H   J

19. How many inches of ribbon are needed to trim the perimeter of the quilt?

   A 125 inches
   B 250 inches
   C   90 inches
   D 180 inches

20. When the quilt is finished, what fraction of it will be green?

   F $\frac{5}{6}$

   G $\frac{2}{3}$

   H $\frac{1}{2}$

   J $\frac{3}{4}$

21. Marcus kept this record of the high temperatures each day for one week: 86°F, 90°F, 94°F, 93°F, 88°F, 85°F, 87°F. What was the average high temperature that week?

   A 91°F
   B 90°F
   C 89°F
   D 88°F

22. Which of these expressions represents the total number of dots in the arrangement shown?

   F $(3 \times 3) + 2$
   G $(3 \div 3) + 2$
   H $(3 \times 5) - 2$
   J $(3 \times 5) + 2$

23. Lulu wants to triple a cookie recipe that calls for $\frac{3}{4}$ cup of molasses. How much molasses should Lulu use?

   A $\frac{9}{12}$ cup

   B $\frac{4}{9}$ cup

   C 4 cups

   D $2\frac{1}{4}$ cups

24. Lulu's cookies must bake for 12 minutes. She puts a sheet of cookies into the oven at 3:54. When should she take it out?

   F 4:06
   G 4:04
   H 3:56
   J 3:42

25. Xavier wants to put a baseboard around the perimeter of his bedroom. The bedroom is 15 feet long and 10 feet wide. How much baseboard does Xavier need?

A 50 feet
B 25 feet
C 150 feet
D 5 feet

The chart below shows the sales tax charged in Central City. Study the table. Then do Questions 26–28.

Sale	Tax	Sale	Tax
$0.00 – $0.11	$0.01	$0.56 – $0.66	$0.06
0.12 – 0.22	0.02	0.67 – 0.77	0.07
0.23 – 0.33	0.03	0.78 – 0.88	0.08
0.34 – 0.44	0.04	0.89 – 0.99	0.09
0.45 – 0.55	0.05		

26. Which of these represents the amount for which tax goes up by one cent?

F 9 cents spent
G 11 cents spent
H 12 cents spent
J 13 cents spent

27. How much tax would there be on a $1.50 purchase?

A 5 cents
B 10 cents
C 14 cents
D 15 cents

28. How much would it cost to buy a bar of candy for 50 cents, plus tax?

F 50 cents
G 51 cents
H 55 cents
J 59 cents

Use this price list to answer Numbers 29–32.

Tent Rental Fees

Tent Size (in feet)	Rate per Day
10 by 10	$15
10 by 15	$22
15 by 20	$37

Pickup and delivery: $25.
Office Hours: 9:30 A.M. to 6:00 P.M., Monday through Friday

29. Which steps describe how to find the cost to rent a 10-by-15-foot tent plus a 15-by-20-foot tent for 3 days?

A Add, then divide.
B Multiply, then subtract.
C Add, then multiply.
D Subtract, then multiply.

30. How much would it cost to rent a 10-by-15-foot tent for 2 days and include pickup and delivery?

F $44   H $47
G $69   J $77

31. How long is the office open each weekday?

A $9\frac{1}{2}$ hr   C $15\frac{1}{2}$ hr

B $8\frac{3}{4}$ hr   D $8\frac{1}{2}$ hr

32. Maria is thinking about renting the 15-by-20-foot tent for her family reunion. If the cost of 1-day rental were split among 9 families, about how much would each family pay?

F $2   H $4
G $3   J $5

33. Germaine's bedroom is 10 ft by 15 ft. Which of these is equal to the measurements of Germaine's bedroom?

    A 3 yd by 4 yd   **C** $3\frac{2}{3}$ yd by 4 yd

    B $3\frac{1}{2}$ yd by 2 yd   **D** $3\frac{1}{3}$ yd by 5 yd

34. What unit would be used to measure the amount of milk needed to make a cake?

    F liters
    G pounds
    H cups
    J milliliters

35. What is the correct value for point P on the number line?

    A 11.25
    B 11.3
    C 12.25
    D 11.15

36. Which of the following is the best estimate for the weight of a pet cat?

    F   1 pound
    G   10 pounds
    H 100 pounds
    J 1,000 pounds

37. What temperature is shown on this thermometer?

    A 33°
    B 37°
    C 34°
    D 35°

38. Kevin was told he would earn three thousand, fifty-six dollars a month at his new job. Which of these numbers represents his monthly salary?

    F $30,056
    G $ 3,560
    H $ 3,056
    J $ 3,506

39. Which pair has the digits 0, 3, 5, and 7 arranged to make the least decimal number and then the greatest decimal number possible?

    A 0.0357 and 0.7530
    B 0.0537 and 0.7530
    C 0.0357 and 0.7350
    D 0.0753 and 0.7530

40. In the list below, *Input* numbers have been changed by a rule to get *Output* numbers. Which of these could be the rule for changing the *Input* numbers to the *Output* numbers?

Input	Output
3	4
6	5
9	6

    F Add 1.
    G Divide by 3. Then add 3.
    H Multiply by 2. Then subtract 2.
    J Add 1. Then subtract 4.

Members of the Blackwood Condominium Association all own apartments in the same building. They put their money together to pay for any building repairs. This graph shows how much the association had in savings each year from 2000 to 2005. Study the graph. Then use it to do Numbers 41–44.

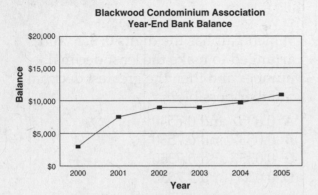

Blackwood Condominium Association Year-End Bank Balance

41. During which two years was the association's bank balance about the same?

A 2001 and 2002
B 2002 and 2003
C 2003 and 2004
D 2004 and 2005

42. Between what two years did the bank balance increase the most?

F 2000 and 2001
G 2001 and 2002
H 2003 and 2004
J 2004 and 2005

43. Which of these is the best estimate of how much the association had in its bank account at the end of 2005?

A $10,000
B $10,500
C $11,000
D $12,000

44. About how much money did the association save between 2000 and 2001?

F $3,000
G $8,000
H $5,000
J $2,000

45. If the same number is used in both boxes, which of these statements is true?

A If ☐ − 6 = 8, then 8 + 6 = ☐.
B If ☐ − 6 = 8, then 8 − 6 = ☐.
C If ☐ − 6 = 8, then 6 − ☐ = 8.
D If ☐ − 6 = 8, then 6 × 8 = ☐.

46. Which of these is an equilateral triangle?

F   G   H   J

47. In the number 70,314, what is the value of the 7?

A   70
B   700
C   7,000
D   70,000

48. What will be the next figure in the pattern?

≋ ▦ ≋ ▦ ≋ ▦ ≋ ▦ ___

F ≋   H ▦

G ▦   J ▨

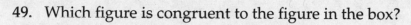

49. Which figure is congruent to the figure in the box?

               A   **B**   **C**   **D**

50. Which diagram shows perpendicular lines?

    1   2   3   4

F 1 only
G 2 and 3 only
H 2 only
J 1 and 2 only

Skills Inventory Posttest Evaluation

Use the answer keys to check your answers on the posttest. The evaluation chart matches each problem in the posttest to a skill area. Use the charts to find which pages in this book to use for help with problems you missed.

Answer Key—Part A

1.	B	14.	H
2.	H	15.	A
3.	E	16.	H
4.	G	17.	B
5.	D	18.	G
6.	H	19.	A
7.	A	20.	H
8.	J	21.	B
9.	B	22.	J
10.	F	23.	E
11.	A	24.	H
12.	K	25.	A
13.	B		

Evaluation Chart—Part A

Problem Number	Skill Area	Text Pages
1, 2, 4, 8, 19	Addition of Whole Numbers	15–21
3, 10, 13, 14	Subtraction of Whole Numbers	26–30
5, 6, 15, 23	Multiplication of Whole Numbers	36–42
7, 9, 16, 22	Division of Whole Numbers	48–58
12, 18, 21	Fractions	63–80, 86
11, 17, 20, 24, 25	Decimals	75–76, 84–93

Answer Key—Part B

1.	C	26.	G
2.	G	27.	C
3.	D	28.	H
4.	H	29.	C
5.	C	30.	G
6.	H	31.	D
7.	C	32.	H
8.	G	33.	D
9.	A	34.	H
10.	G	35.	B
11.	C	36.	G
12.	J	37.	B
13.	D	38.	H
14.	H	39.	B
15.	A	40.	G
16.	J	41.	B
17.	C	42.	F
18.	H	43.	C
19.	D	44.	H
20.	H	45.	A
21.	C	46.	H
22.	F	47.	D
23.	D	48.	F
24.	F	49.	C
25.	A	50.	J

Evaluation Chart—Part B

Problem Number	Skill Area	Text Pages
3, 4, 8, 12, 17, 20, 23, 29, 35, 38, 39, 45, 47	Number and Number Operations	8–12, 15–20, 26–30, 36–42, 48–54, 56–58, 120
6, 11, 13, 16, 28	Computation in Context	44–45, 59–60, 93, 139
7, 32, 36, 43, 44	Estimation	12, 21, 31–32, 43, 55, 65, 74, 92
19, 24, 25, 31, 33, 34, 37	Measurement	124–140
14, 46, 48, 49, 50	Geometry and Spatial Sense	110, 143–154
10, 27, 30, 41, 42	Data Analysis	98–99, 102–106
21	Statistics and Probability	100–101, 107
1, 2, 5, 15, 18, 40	Patterns, Functions, Algebra	110–121
9, 22, 26	Problem Solving and Reasoning	22–23, 32–33, 44–45, 59–60, 93, 139, 155

Answer Key

The Number System

Page 8

1. thousands; 4,000
2. hundreds; 400
3. thousands; 4,000
4. ten thousands; 40,000
5. tens; 40
6. ten thousands; 40,000
7. ones; 4
8. tens; 40
9. ten millions; 40,000,000
10. hundred thousands; 400,000
11. millions; 4,000,000
12. hundred millions; 400,000,000

Page 9

1. 10,000 + 3,000 + 200 + 50 + 6
2. 400,000 + 80,000 + 1,000 + 500 + 4
3. 6,000 + 10 + 3
4. 900,000 + 7,000 + 300 + 30 + 4
5. 10,457
6. 208,543
7. 1,007,096
8. 43,670

Page 10

1. C
2. H
3. A
4. G
5. C

6. G
7. 6,012
8. 806,183
9. 140,065
10. 17,017,070

Page 11

1. 2,842
2. 193
3. 21,403
4. 98
5. 876
6. 12,705
7. 20,000
8. 51
9. 11,000
10. 160
11. 13
12. 1,720
13. 52, 97, 115, 146
14. 9, 17, 95, 103
15. 178, 203, 517, 695, 961
16. 127
17. 678
18. 932
19. 8,542

Page 12

1. 380
2. 1,450
3. 40
4. 10
5. 300
6. 100
7. 500
8. 12,100

Number System Skills Checkup

Pages 13–14

1. C
2. H
3. D
4. G
5. C
6. J
7. D
8. F
9. C
10. J
11. A
12. F
13. D
14. J
15. C

Addition

Page 15

1. 19 + 12 = 31
   31 − 19 = 12
   31 − 12 = 19
2. B
3. False.
4. 423

Page 16

Row 1. 5, 6, 14, 3
Row 2. 16, 10, 4, 15
Row 3. 2, 11, 9, 4
Row 4. 7, 11, 0, 5
Row 5. 7, 15, 8, 17, 18, 4
Row 6. 7, 12, 8, 6, 3, 3

Row 7. 6, 8, 8, 12, 12, 10
Row 8. 10, 11, 2, 9, 9, 5
Row 9. 13, 10, 15, 7, 8, 0
Row 10. 13, 12, 16, 6, 13, 13

Page 17
Row 1. 63, 19, 10, 18¢, 39, 287
Row 2. 167, 39 yd, 136, 11, 12, 15 in.
Row 3. 16, 15, 38, 58, $170, 95
Row 4. 119 in., 78, 19, $13.68, 108, 585

Page 18
1. 94
2. 682
3. 165
4. $85.75
5. 1,978
6. 998
7. 181
8. 739
9. 817
10. 6,554
11. 5,460
12. 578
13. 198
14. 198
15. 199
16. 765

Page 19
Row 1. 66; 118; 70; 190; 1,125

Row 2. 271 gal; 11,502; 107 cans; 272 in.; 120
Row 3. 225 mi; 5,928; 216; 919 in.; 818
Row 4. 520, $40.50, 240, 732, 323

Page 20
5. $35
6. 231
7. $1.90
8. 701
9. 1,200
10. $125
11. $2.40
12. 3,110
13. 530
14. $8.25
15. 622
16. 452
17. 5,100
18. 7,222

Page 21
Row 1. 13,000; 11,000; 160 yd; $70
Row 2. 800; 30,000; 5,000; 200
3. D
4. H
5. B
6. F
7. A
8. H

Page 22
1. How much space will be left between the end of his bed and the other wall?
2. Circled; How many people in all work at the Busy Bee during rush hour?
3. Circled; How many geese is that in all?
4. How many games can you play for $5?
5. How far under the speed limit is he driving?
6. Circled; What was the total cost?
7. Circled; What is the least number of parking spaces the lot must have?
8. Circled; How much money did she have after she subtracted the cost of the bingo cards?
9. 273
10. $8.90
11. $5.95
12. $8
13. How much did the shirt cost?
14. What did the cat weigh last year?
15. What was the cost without the air conditioning?
16. How much was the payment before it went up?

Addition Skills Checkup

Pages 24–25

1. D
2. G
3. A
4. J
5. E
6. J
7. C
8. G
9. B
10. H
11. A
12. G
13. E
14. H
15. B
16. H
17. D
18. G
19. D

Subtraction

Page 26

1. F
2. T
3. T
4. T

Page 27

Row 1.   2, 4, 5
Row 2.   2, 8, 3
Row 3.   9, 1, 3
Row 4.   3, 3, 1

Row 5.   1, 1, 0, 1, 6, 4, 0
Row 6.   6, 2, 2, 2, 1, 3, 5
Row 7.   4, 4, 6, 4, 1, 7, 6
Row 8.   6, 5, 8, 7, 1, 5, 4
Row 9.   5, 3, 8, 3, 2, 4, 0

Page 28

1. 250
2. 431
3. 7,410
4. 11 miles
5. 516
6. 1,343
7. 2,300
8. 30
9. $2.13
10. 1,124
11. $10
12. 54 in.
13. $2.27
14. 462

Page 29

1. 74
2. 127
3. 592
4. $0.72
5. 26
6. 1,533 meters
7. 1,037 feet
8. $11.25
9. $1.25
10. 863
11. 3,061
12. 683
13. 906
14. 309

15. 919
16. $1.29

Page 30

17. 297
18. 792
19. 129
20. 328
21. 77
22. 1,059
23. 366
24. 3,044
25. 5,136
26. 378
27. 3,139
28. 378
29. 1,059
30. 548
31. 5,076

Page 31

1. $10
2. $300
3. 22,000
4. $30
5. 50,000
6. 800
7. 2,000
8. 1,000
9. 60,000
10. $30
11. 7,000
12. 400 feet
13. $19 − $13 = $6
14. $76 − $39 = $37
15. $62 − $40 = $22
16. $7 − $3 = $4

17. $40 - $10 = $30
18. $300 - $50 = $250

Page 32

1. C; $7
2. J; 100 bags
3. B; 35 pounds
4. H; 20 days
5. A; 14 inches
6. G; $295

Page 33

7. 511
8. 20
9. 333
10. 50
11. How much did he start with?
12. How much does the dining room set cost?
13. How much cement will be used for the patio?
14. How long does the drive usually take?

Subtraction Skills Checkup

Pages 34–35

1. D
2. F
3. A
4. H
5. D
6. F
7. D
8. J

9. C
10. J
11. A
12. G
13. B
14. F
15. D
16. F
17. C
18. F
19. B
20. F

Multiplication

Page 36

1. T
2. F
3. T
4. T
5. T
6. T
7. T
8. T
9. T
10. T

Page 37

Row 1.   12, 16, 27, 56
Row 2.   6, 32, 36, 54
Row 3.   30, 15, 42, 36
Row 4.   8, 28, 72, 48
Row 5.   12, 4, 21, 27
Row 6.   49, 24, 9, 20
Row 7.   45, 35, 14, 24
Row 8.   16, 18, 40, 64

Row 9.   36, 56, 25, 48
Row 10. 63, 18, 81, 54

Page 38

Row 1.   48, 696, $4.88, 155, 246 in.
Row 2.   408; 405 ft; $9; 148; 2,760
3. 428
4. 129
5. 350
6. 4,050
7. 99
8. $8.26
9. $18.88
10. 21,009
11. $64

Page 39

1. 160
2. 260
3. 1,230
4. 195
5. 224
6. 575
7. 220
8. 1,008
9. 3,655
10. 57
11. 168
12. 942
13. 1,232
14. 140
15. 570
16. 4,963
17. 125
18. 729

Page 40

1. 36, 45, 54, 63, 72
2. 100, 125, 150, 175, 200
3. 80, 100, 120, 140, 160
4. 44, 55, 66, 77, 88
5. 28, 35, 42, 49, 56
6. B
7. F
8. C
9. J
10. T
11. F
12. T
13. T
14. F
15. T

Page 41

1. 80
2. 400
3. 480
4. 470
5. 1,500
6. 2,800
7. 180
8. 5,600
9. 1,000
10. 180
11. 5,600
12. 1,000
13. 270
14. 2,700
15. 5,600
16. 300
17. 4,680
18. 46,800
19. 6,000

20. 1,200
21. 12,300
22. 3,000
23. 9,990
24. 99,900

Page 42

Row 1.   143; 2,662; 3,926; 525; 903

Row 2.   20,800; 9,150; 2,880; 1,953; 1,045

3. 6,930
4. 16,416
5. 2,130
6. 6,946
7. 968
8. 2,550
9. 19,800
10. 3,200
11. 9,460

Page 43

1. 700
2. 3,000
3. 18,000
4. $90
5. $50 to $65
6. 1,800 feet
7. $500
8. 35,000
9. 6,400
10. 54,000
11. 48,000
12. 3,600

Page 44

1. C
2. H
3. C
4. F
5. B
6. H

Page 45

7. What size car did he rent?
8. How many people were there?
9. How many square feet are there?
10. $128
11. 26
12. 105
13. 400

Multiplication Skills Checkup

Pages 46−47

1. B
2. G
3. C
4. F
5. E
6. K
7. B
8. J
9. B
10. H
11. B
12. G
13. A

14. J
15. C
16. J
17. B
18. H
19. A
20. J
21. D

Division

Page 48
1. 671
2. 0
3. 1
4. 15
5. 9
6. 1

Page 49
Row 1.   2, 4, 2, 3
Row 2.   2, 8, 6, 5
Row 3.   6, 5, 3, 4
Row 4.   5, 7, 2, 3
Row 5.   4, 2, 7, 9
Row 6.   7, 8, 7, 7
Row 7.   9, 5, 2, 4
Row 8.   8, 9, 8, 8
Row 9.   9, 7, 5, 6
Row 10. 7, 6, 9, 6

Page 50
1. $5\overline{)70}$
2. $2\overline{)98}$
3. $12\overline{)24}$
4. $12\overline{)142}$
5. $10\overline{)150}$
6. $25\overline{)575}$
7. $15\overline{)90}$
8. $9\overline{)81}$
9. $4\overline{)212}$
10. $2\overline{)98}$
11. $4\overline{)16}$
12. $5\overline{)\$20}$
13. $3\overline{)1,200}$
14. $3\overline{)\$654}$
15. $12\overline{)250}$
16. $12\overline{)24}$

Pages 51–52
1. 21
2. 32
3. 134
4. 11 inches
5. 112
6. 412
7. 224
8. $132
9. 121
10. 332
11. 322
12. 231
13. 101
14. 201
15. 204
16. 210
17. 110
18. 402
19. 302
20. 230

21. 82
22. 41
23. 80
24. 60
25. 32
26. 60
27. 51
28. 80
29. 41
30. 21
31. 50
32. 61

Page 53
1. 2 R2
2. 7 R3
3. 8 R1
4. 2 R5
5. 5 R2
6. 7 R5
7. 4 R2
8. 4 R3
9. 9 R2
10. 5 R3
11. 5 R5
12. 6 R1
13. 9 R1
14. 7 R3
15. 8 R3
16. 9 R4
17. 7 R1
18. 7 R1

Page 54
1. 105
2. 109
3. 109

4. 104
5. 406
6. 203
7. 209
8. 103
9. 209
10. 105
11. 102
12. 105
13. 303
14. 903
15. 308
16. 205

Page 55

1. 400
2. 60
3. 100
4. 100
5. 200
6. 300
7. 200
8. 1,000
9. 200
10. 200
11. C
12. J
13. B
14. F
15. A

Page 56

1. 25
2. 29
3. 13
4. 27
5. 12

6. 14
7. 14
8. 37
9. 52
10. 55
11. 68
12. 112
13. 115
14. 131
15. 62

Page 57

1. 135
2. 22
3. 144
4. 22
5. 1,781 R1
6. 1,652 R1
7. 776
8. 750 R3
9. 1,031
10. 1,875
11. 503 R1
12. 696

Page 58

1. 2
2. 3
3. 14
4. 31
5. 30
6. 5
7. 4
8. 5 R7
9. 6 R8
10. 63 R5
11. 15 R5

12. 6 R7
13. 4
14. 4 R30
15. 50 R40
16. 55 R4

Page 59

1. B
2. J
3. D
4. H
5. What was the cost of cable service?
6. How many widgets are there?

Page 60

1. B
2. H
3. C
4. F
5. B
6. G

Division Skills Checkup

Pages 61–62

1. B
2. J
3. D
4. H
5. A
6. H
7. A
8. H
9. D

10. G
11. D
12. G
13. B
14. K
15. C
16. F
17. C
18. G
19. D
20. G

Fractions

Page 64

1. A
2. H
3. D
4. H
5. D
6. H

Page 65

1. 4, 20
2. 2, 8
3. 3, $\frac{12}{15}$
4. $\frac{1}{6}$, $\frac{5}{30}$
5. 9
6. 10
7. 24
8. 5
9. 2, 7
10. 5, 3
11. 12, $\frac{2}{3}$

12. $\frac{2}{2}$, 6
13. 7
14. 10
15. 9
16. 1

Page 66

Factors

10	1, 2, 5, 10
12	1, 2, 3, 4, 6, 12
15	1, 3, 5, 15
16	1, 2, 4, 8, 16
18	1, 2, 3, 6, 9, 18
20	1, 2, 4, 5, 10, 20

1. $\frac{1}{3}$
2. $\frac{2}{3}$
3. $\frac{4}{5}$
4. $\frac{1}{3}$
5. $\frac{1}{3}$
6. $\frac{1}{6}$
7. $\frac{2}{5}$
8. $\frac{3}{4}$

Page 67

1. 3
2. 8
3. 10
4. 7
5. 1
6. 12

7. G
8. 12
9. 10
10. 27
11. 10
12. 16
13. 20
14. G

Page 68

1. 5
2. 6
3. 22
4. 20
5. 2
6. $1\frac{1}{8}$
7. $1\frac{3}{5}$
8. $3\frac{2}{5}$

Page 69

1. >
2. <
3. >
4. <
5. $\frac{2}{5}$, $\frac{4}{5}$, $\frac{5}{5}$, $\frac{7}{5}$
6. $\frac{1}{5}$, $\frac{1}{4}$, $\frac{1}{3}$, $\frac{1}{2}$
7. $1\frac{1}{5}$, $1\frac{1}{3}$, $1\frac{1}{2}$
8. $\frac{3}{5} > \frac{3}{7}$; Graham
9. Wednesday
10. Ahmed

Page 70

11. $<$; LCM = 12
12. $=$; LCM = 12
13. $<$; LCM = 10
14. $<$
15. $=$
16. $>$
17. $>$
18. $>$
19. $<$

Page 71

1. $\frac{5}{6}$
2. $\frac{1}{2}$
3. $1\frac{1}{5}$
4. $\frac{1}{6}$
5. $1\frac{1}{7}$
6. $1\frac{5}{9}$
7. $\frac{5}{9}$
8. $\frac{1}{2}$
9. $\frac{1}{15}$
10. $\frac{1}{2}$
11. 1
12. $\frac{4}{5}$
13. $\frac{5}{8}$
14. $\frac{2}{5}$
15. 0

16. $1\frac{2}{5}$
17. $\frac{1}{3}$
18. 1

Page 72

1. $\frac{1}{6}$
2. $\frac{5}{21}$
3. 1
4. $\frac{1}{8}$
5. $\frac{1}{12}$
6. 15
7. 5
8. $\frac{9}{64}$
9. 5
10. $\frac{1}{4}$
11. $\frac{3}{20}$
12. $\frac{1}{24}$
13. $\frac{1}{6}$
14. $\frac{1}{10}$
15. 1
16. $\frac{1}{14}$
17. $\frac{1}{12}$
18. 8
19. 4
20. 14

Page 73

1. $\frac{5}{21}$
2. $\frac{12}{17}$
3. $\frac{7}{20}$
4. $\frac{2}{15}$
5. 9
6. $\frac{3}{20}$
7. $1\frac{1}{3}$
8. $\frac{1}{6}$
9. $\frac{3}{5}$
10. $\frac{1}{20}$
11. $\frac{2}{21}$
12. $\frac{1}{7}$

Page 74

1. 3
2. 6
3. 1
4. 9
5. 26
6. 2
7. $2 + 2 = 4$
8. $5 \times 3 = 15$
9. $10 \quad 5 = 5$

Page 75

1. 0.6
2. $0.166\ldots$, or $0.1\overline{6}$
3. 0.05
4. 0.1

5. $0.222\ldots$, or $0.\overline{2}$
6. $0.666\ldots$, or $0.\overline{6}$
7. $0.444\ldots$, or $0.\overline{4}$
8. 0.007
9. 0.75
10. 0.17
11. 0.5
12. 0.9

Page 76

1. $\frac{4}{5}$
2. $\frac{7}{10}$
3. $\frac{3}{4}$
4. $2\frac{2}{5}$
5. $\frac{9}{10}$
6. $\frac{3}{20}$
7. $1\frac{4}{5}$
8. $5\frac{1}{5}$
9. $3\frac{3}{50}$
10. $\frac{21}{100}$
11. $7\frac{3}{10}$
12. $\frac{3}{5}$

Page 77

1. $\frac{3}{4} > \frac{1}{2}$; too long
2. $\frac{1}{2}$ pound

3. Yes. $\frac{5}{2}$ yd $= 2\frac{1}{2}$ yd
4. $\frac{2}{3}$
5. $\frac{22}{125}$
6. $\frac{1}{4}$
7. $1\frac{1}{2}$ inches
8. 1 inch
9. $\frac{1}{4}$ foot
10. The crystal baby is taller.
11. 1 cup
12. $\frac{1}{2}$ cup

Page 78

2. $\dfrac{\text{teachers}}{\text{students}}\ \dfrac{2}{31}$
3. $\dfrac{\text{miles driven}}{\text{minutes of rest}}\ \dfrac{100}{15} = \dfrac{20}{3}$
4. $\dfrac{\text{quarts}}{\text{gallons}}\ \dfrac{4}{1}$
5. $\dfrac{\text{miles}}{\text{gallons}}\ \dfrac{22}{1}$
6. $\dfrac{\text{dollars}}{\text{family}}\ \dfrac{12}{1}$
7. $\dfrac{\text{minutes}}{\text{box}}\ \dfrac{20}{1}$
8. $\dfrac{\text{dollars}}{\text{hours}}\ \dfrac{10}{1}$

Page 79

1. $=$
2. $\neq$
3. $=$
4. $\neq$
5. $=$

6. $\neq$
7. $=$
8. $\neq$
9. $=$
10. $\neq$
11. $\neq$
12. $\neq$

Page 80

1. $\dfrac{\text{boxes}}{\text{hours}}\ \dfrac{4}{1} = \dfrac{32}{8}$
2. $\dfrac{\text{sheets}}{\text{books}}\ \dfrac{64}{1} = \dfrac{448}{7}$
3. $\dfrac{\text{red}}{\text{yellow}}\ \dfrac{1}{3} = \dfrac{8}{24}$
4. $\dfrac{\text{miles}}{\text{gallons}}\ \dfrac{15}{1} = \dfrac{75}{5}$
5. Yes.
6. Yes.
7. Yes.
8. Yes.

Page 81

1. 48
2. 8
3. 24
4. 39
5. 18
6. 36
7. 28
8. 16
9. $\frac{50}{1} = \frac{n}{3}$; 150 miles
10. $\frac{15}{1} = \frac{150}{n}$; 10 months
11. $\frac{2}{3} = \frac{n}{15}$; 10 days
12. $\frac{1}{3} = \frac{n}{18}$; 6 pounds

Fractions Skills Checkup

Pages 82–83

1. D
2. J
3. C
4. K
5. A
6. G
7. C
8. G
9. D
10. J
11. A
12. G
13. D
14. H
15. C
16. K
17. C
18. J
19. C
20. J
21. C
22. J
23. A

Decimals

Page 84

1. 6
2. 9
3. 6
4. 3
5. 2
6. 0

7. 6
8. 5
9. 7
10. 2
11. 6
12. 3
13. tenths
14. thousandths
15. hundredths
16. ones
17. thousandths
18. tenths
19. ones
20. hundredths

Page 85

1. D
2. B
3. F
4. C
5. E
6. A
7. six tenths
8. one hundredth
9. three and five hundredths
10. ten and one tenth
11. one hundred twenty-five thousandths
12. forty and one hundred thousandths

Page 86

1. 0.3; $\frac{3}{10}$
2. 0.09; $\frac{9}{100}$

3. 1.00; $\frac{100}{100}$
4. 1.0; $\frac{10}{10}$
5. $\frac{24}{1,000}$; 0.024
6. $\frac{19}{100}$; 0.19
7. $\frac{100}{100}$; 1.00
8. $\frac{909}{1,000}$; 0.909
9. $1\frac{6}{10}$; 1.6
10. $3\frac{3}{100}$; 3.03

Page 87

1. 7, 70, 0.7, 0.70
2. 40, 400, 0.40, 0.400
3. not equal
4. equal
5. equal
6. not equal
7. equal
8. equal
9. equal
10. not equal
11. equal

Page 88

1. 0.003
2. 0.098
3. 0.00899
4. 1.032
5. 0.13
6. 0.005
7. 0.09
8. 0.19
9. 1.05

10. 0.002
11. 0.01, 0.1, 1, 11
12. 0.023, 0.032, 0.15, 0.75
13. 0.75, 2.3, 8.7
14. 0.37, 0.73, 3.07, 30.7
15. 0.9531
16. 0.8731

Page 89

1. 8.6; 0.46; $2.60; 1.14; 2.62; 1.03
2. 3.19
3. 0.198
4. 6.238
5. 0.19
6. 6.012
7. 52.95
8. 5.264
9. 1.82
10. 23.115

Page 90

1. 2.9; 0.03; $7.25; 0.05; 1.38; 7.48
2. 0.1
3. 6.47
4. 0.122
5. 17.3
6. 0.74
7. 0.84
8. 0.743
9. 3.43
10. 0.06
11. 11.187
12. 3.444
13. 13.46

Page 91

1. 0.18
2. 0.26
3. $27.00
4. $2.25
5. 0.75
6. 1.525
7. $49.95
8. $0.45
9. 0.036
10. 0.084
11. 2.1
12. 0.3
13. 0.042
14. 0.062
15. 0.0045

Page 92

1. 1
2. 12
3. 25
4. 4
5. 7
6. 180
7. 9
8. 3
9. 301
10. $25
11. 0.8
12. 7.2
13. 0.1
14. 0.0
15. 0.2
16. 9.8
17. 32.0
18. 1.0

19. 9.9
20. No. 15.3 < 15.5

Page 93

1. C
2. H
3. 27.6 feet
4. 37.5 pounds
5. 211.96 inches
6. 421.3 miles

Decimals Skills Checkup

Pages 94–95

1. E
2. H
3. C
4. H
5. C
6. J
7. C
8. G
9. C
10. H
11. A
12. H
13. B
14. H
15. C
16. F
17. D
18. J
19. D
20. H
21. A
22. J

Data Analysis

Pages 96–97
1. D
2. G
3. C
4. F
5. $2
6. $6.50
7. $5.25
8. regular video for 1 day
9. new release
10. $5
11. new releases
12. $13
13. C

Page 98
1. Linda
2. David
3. 5 years
4. Anne
5. Myumi
6. 15 years
7. Tubman
8. Roosevelt
9. 2 times

Page 99
1. $1.60
2. $11.40
3. $2.90
4. $4.10
5. $6.50
6. $9.70
7. 6
8. 75¢

Page 101

Median	Mode	Mean
2.5	2	3
4	none	4
2	2	2
6	5, 6	6

2. median 3, mode 2
3. median 23, mode 23
4. median 65, mode 78
5. median $12.25, mode $12
6. 40
7. 5 miles
8. $75
9. 9

Page 103
1. C
2. G
3. D
4. J
5. D
6. F
7. A
8. G

Page 104
1. students
2. unemployed
3. 4,000
4. 12,000
5. C
6. H
7. C
8. G

Page 105
1. 3.0
2. 4.0
3. increase
4. 1 grade level
5. Student B
6. Student E
7. Students A and D
8. Student C

Page 106
1. 5 minutes
2. May 10 and 11
3. 5 minutes
4. May 16
5. 5 minutes
6. C
7. G
8. Yes. There is a continuing rise.

Page 107
1. C
2. J
3. C
4. J
5. A
6. G

Data Analysis Skills Checkup

Pages 108–109
1. C
2. G
3. D
4. G

5. B
6. G
7. B
8. G
9. A
10. G
11. A
12. J
13. B

Algebra

Pages 110–111

1. C
2. G
3. C
4. F
5. B
6. 2 circles, 1 bar, 1 X
7. A
8. ,
9.
10. ,
11. ,

Page 112

1. 7, 4, 1
2. 21, 27, 33
3. 18, 23, 28
4. 16, 32, 64
5. 15, 31, 63

6. 176; 527; 1,580
7. 4
8. 11
9. 3
10. 3
11. plus 7
12. plus 15
13. minus 5
14. minus 6
15. 18
16. 35, 20
17. 8
18. 16
19. 7

Page 113

1. +
2. −
3. ×
4. +
5. +
6. −
7. ÷
8. ÷
9. +
10. −
11. ÷
12. ×
13. 4
14. 8
15. 10
16. 12
17. 4
18. 9
19. 12
20. 22
21. 2

22. 10
23. 12
24. 3

Page 115

1. ÷
2. −
3. +
4. 520
5. 0
6. 1
7. y
8. T
9. F
10. T
11. T
12. T
13. F
14. T

Page 116

1. In 55; Out 15, 75
2. In 3; Out 12, 300
3. In 10; Out 0, 5
4. C
5. H
6. Subtract 2.
7. Add 10.
8. Multiply by 5.
9. Add 12.
10. Divide by 4.

Page 117

1. D
2. F
3. C

4. G
5. $n + 24$
6. $n + 6$
7. $n - 7$
8. $\frac{n}{2}$ or $\times \frac{1}{2} n$
9. $n + 8$
10. $6 \times n$
11. $\frac{13}{n}$ or $13 \div n$
12. $n - 6$
13. $14 \times n$
14. $n + 10$

Page 118

15. $r + \$20$
16. $\frac{p}{4}$ or $p \div 4$
17. $n - \$450$
18. $3 \times c$
19. $d + m$
20. $4 \times k$
21. $28 - d$
22. $6 - f$
23. $y - 7$
24. $172 - x$

Page 119

1. D
2. F
3. A
4. H
5. C
6. 10
7. 8
8. 13
9. 5
10. 25

11. 4
12. 9
13. 17
14. 8

Page 120

1. B
2. J
3. G
4. $24 - 7 = x$
5. $9,000 + x = 12,000$
6. $7 + 3 = x$

Page 121

1. 8
2. 25
3. 15
4. 25
5. 39
6. 40
7. 15
8. 103

Algebra Skills Checkup

Pages 122–123

1. D
2. H
3. A
4. F
5. B
6. F
7. D
8. H
9. B

10. F
11. C
12. F
13. D
14. J
15. B
16. H
17. C
18. H
19. D
20. G

Measurement

Page 124

2. length, miles
3. area, square feet
4. capacity, gallons
5. weight, ounces
6. temperature, degrees
7. length, yards
8. volume, cubic feet

Page 125

1. A
2. D
3. F
4. H
5. A
6. F
7. B
8. H
9. C

Page 126

1. 14,000 lbs
2. 15 yd
3. 6 ft
4. 4 pt
5. $\frac{1}{2}$ lb
6. 4 hr
7. 13 wk
8. $\frac{2}{3}$ yd
9. 168 hr
10. 6 qt

Page 127

11. 15 ft
12. 6,000 lb
13. $\frac{1}{2}$ ft
14. $4\frac{1}{2}$ C
15. 144 in.
16. $1\frac{1}{2}$ ft
17. 21,600 sec
18. 35 wks
19. 96 oz
20. $\frac{1}{3}$ yd
21. 6 pt
22. $\frac{1}{8}$ T

Page 128

1. 100 cm
2. 1,000 m
3. 1 g
4. 1 L
5. 100 g
6. 1,000 L

7. 1 dm
8. 1,000 mm
9. 1 kg

Page 129

1. 500,000 mg
2. 100,000 cm
3. 2 L
4. 250 mg
5. 3.7 L
6. 12,500 m
7. 0.01 L
8. 400 dkg
9. 0.3 m
10. 2,500 g

Page 130

1. 6 ft 2 in.
2. 3 yd 2 ft
3. 2 lb 1 oz
4. 4 qt
5. 1 L 225 mL or 1.225 L
6. 3 ft 3 in.
7. 11 fl oz
8. 3 ft 10 in.
9. 3 yd 7 in.
10. 18 cg 5 mg or 18.5 cg
11. 11 oz
12. 1 qt 1 pt
13. 1 km 859 m or 1.859 km
14. 7 mo
15. 1,450 lb

Page 131

1. B
2. H

3. B
4. F
5. B
6. J

Page 132

1. A
2. G
3. C
4. J
5. B
6. H

Page 133

1. 2
2. 2
3. 4
4. 10
5. 25
6. 75
7. 5
8. 15
9. 150
10. 95
11. 40

Page 134

1. degrees Fahrenheit
2. 32ºF
3. colder
4. D
5. G
6. 1ºC
7. 2ºC, 2ºF
8. 36ºC, 96ºF
9. B

Page 135

1. 34 ft
2. 30 mi
3. 30 in.
4. 10'
5. 8 cm
6. 22'
7. 16 ft
8. 2 cm

Page 136

1. 36 cm²
2. 8 mm²
3. 50 mi²
4. 36 in²
5. 4 ft²
6. 4 cm²
7. 18 m²
8. 5 in.

Page 137

1. A, C
2. F, J
3. C
4. J
5. 30 min
6. 120 min
7. 20 min
8. 48 hrs
9. 90 min
10. 45 min

Page 138

1. 9:00
2. 3:00
3. 11:00
4. 4:20
5. 1.45
6. 1:45

Page 139

1. 5 hr 5 min
2. 3 hrs 45 min
3. 4 hrs 25 min
4. 6 hrs 5 min
5. 50 min
6. 6 hrs 20 min

Page 140

1. 5 hrs 45 min
2. 1 hr 30 min
3. 6 hrs 20 min
4. 9 hrs
5. 5 hrs 24 min
6. 2 hrs 35 min
7. 2 hrs 50 min
8. 2 hrs 35 min
9. 45 min
10. 1 hr 45 min

Measurement Skills Checkup

Pages 141–142

1. D
2. H
3. B
4. H
5. A
6. H
7. A
8. F
9. B
10. J
11. A
12. G
13. C
14. J
15. C
16. H
17. C
18. H
19. C
20. G

Geometry

Page 143

1. ray *ST*
2. line segment *GH* or *HG*
3. line *KL* or *LK*
4. line *XY* or *YX*
5. ray *MN*
6. line segment *EF* or *FE*

Page 144

1. C
2. F
3. D
4. H
5. A
6. F

Page 145

1. B, E, F, G, H
2. A, C, D
3. F, H

4. Avenue A and Oak
Avenue B and Oak

5. Avenues A and B

Page 146

1. A, D, K
2. B, C, F, G, I, L
3. E, M
4. J
5. F
6. E, F, J, N
7. H
8. N

Page 147

1. A, B, F, G
2. A, F
3. C, E
4. B, F
5. True
6. True
7. True
8. True
9. True
10. True

Page 148

1. 45°, right
2. 110°, obtuse
3. 30°, obtuse
4. 50°, acute
5. right and scalene
6. acute and isosceles
7. obtuse and isosceles
8. obtuse and scalene

Page 149

1. any 2: $\overline{AC}$, $\overline{CD}$, $\overline{EC}$, $\overline{CB}$
2. $\overline{ED}$, $\overline{EB}$
3. $\overline{EB}$
4. $\overline{ED}$
5. 4 in.
6. 6 cm
7. cannot tell
8. 50 mm
9. cannot tell
10. $1\frac{1}{2}$ cm

Page 150

1. B
2. H
3. A
4. F
5. A

Page 151

1. D
2. F
3. D
4. H
5. A
6. H
7. A, M, Y
8. H, X

Page 152

1. C
2. G
3. A
4. B

5. F
6. A and B

Page 153

1. B
2. G
3. B
4. Yes.
5. No.
6. D
7. C

Page 154

1. rectangular solid
2. cylinder
3. cube
4. cone
5. cylinder
6. rectangular solid
7. cylinder
8. 24 in.³
9. No.
10. cylinder

Page 155

1. 4
2. C
3. B
4. 5
5. B
6. H
7. D
8. J

Geometry Skills Checkup

Pages 156–157

1. B
2. G
3. C
4. H
5. A
6. G
7. C
8. J
9. D
10. F
11. D
12. G

Glossary

acute angle   an angle that is less than 90°

acute triangle   a triangle with three acute angles

addends   numbers that are added together to find a sum or total. Example: In the number sentence 7 + 8 = 15, 7 and 8 are addends.

algebra   a branch of mathematics in which letters and symbols are used to represent numbers and relationships

angle   the figure formed by two rays extending from the same point

area   the size of a surface. Area is measured in square units.

average   a typical representation of a group of numbers found by adding the amounts and dividing their sum by the number of amounts that were added together. Also known as the mean.

bar graph   a way of displaying data that uses either horizontal or vertical bars

capacity   a measure of the amount a container can hold when filled

chord   a line segment that connects two points on the circumference of a circle

circle   a flat closed figure that is round in which all points are the same distance from the center point

circle graph   a graph in which a circle is divided into wedges or slices that represent the data. Also known as a pie graph.

circumference   the distance around a circle

cone   a solid that has a flat circular base and a curved surface that ends at a point or vertex

congruent   exactly the same size and shape

cross products   a method of testing whether two fractions or ratios are equal by multiplying the numerator of one fraction and the denominator of a second. Example: $\frac{3}{5} \overset{?}{=} \frac{6}{10}$ The cross products are $3 \times 10 = 6 \times 5$.

customary system   a system of measurement used in the United States. This system includes units such as inches, feet, yards to measure length; ounces and pounds for weight; pints, quarts, and gallons for capacity; and degrees Fahrenheit for temperature.

cylinder   a solid shape with two congruent bases that are circles. The bases are the same distance from one another at all points.

data   information

decimal (fraction)   a number less than 1 written using place value and a decimal point

decimal point   a period used in decimal numbers to separate whole numbers from amounts less than 1

denominator   the bottom number of a fraction that tells the number of equal parts in the whole

diameter   a chord that passes through the center of a circle and connects two points on the circumference

difference   the result of subtracting one amount from another. Example: In the number sentence 15 − 7 = 8, the difference is 8.

dividend   in a division problem, the number that is being divided. Example: In the problem 30 ÷ 6, the dividend is 30.

divisible   a number is divisible by another if the quotient is a whole number and there is no remainder. Example: 15 is divisible by 5. 15 is also divisible by 3, by 15, and by 1.

divisor   in a division problem, the number that you are dividing by. Example: In the problem 30 ÷ 6, the divisor is 6.

edge a line or curve where surfaces of a solid meet

equation a mathematical sentence that shows values that are equal. Example: $3 + 5 = 8$

equilateral triangle a triangle with three equal sides and three equal angles

equivalent equal in value. Example: 0.5 is equivalent to $\frac{1}{2}$.

equivalent fractions fractions that have different numerators and denominators but are equal in value. Example: $\frac{1}{2}$ and $\frac{4}{8}$ are equivalent fractions.

estimate to find an amount that is close to the actual answer. Also, a number that is close to the actual answer.

expanded form a way to write numbers to show the value of each digit

factor a number or letter that is multiplied by another number or letter to yield a product. Example: In the number sentence $3 \times 4 = 12$, both 3 and 4 are factors.

fraction a number representing part of something written in the form $\frac{a}{b}$, where the denominator b represents the number of equal parts in the whole, and the numerator a represents the number of equal parts named

function relationship of exactly one output for every input. Also, a rule.

geometry a branch of mathematics that deals with points, lines, angles, shapes, and solids

improper fraction a fraction in which the numerator is greater than the denominator. Example: $\frac{8}{5}$

inverse operations operations that are opposites of one another and can undo each other. Addition is the inverse of subtraction $(3 + 5 = 8$, and $8 - 3 = 5)$. Multiplication is the inverse of division $(2 \times 3 = 6$, and $6 \div 2 = 3)$

isosceles triangle a triangle with at least two equal sides and angles

key an explanation of symbols or abbreviations

line a set of straight connected points that extends without end in two directions

line graph a graph that uses line segments to connect points that represent data. Line graphs are used to show change over a period of time.

line of symmetry a line that divides a figure into two parts that look exactly alike but face in opposite directions

line segment two points and the straight line between them

lowest terms simplest terms

mass the amount of matter in an object. Also, the term for weight in the metric system.

mean average

median the middle number in a set of numbers that are arranged in order from least to greatest. Example: In the set 12, 15, 16, 19, 21, the median is 16.

metric system a decimal system of measurement in which the meter is the basic unit of length, the gram is the basic unit of mass, and the liter is the basic unit of capacity.

mixed number a number that is made up of a whole number and a fraction. A mixed number represents an amount between two whole numbers. Example: $2\frac{1}{3}$

multiples products of a given number and a whole number. For example, multiples of 3 are 3, 6, 9, 12, and so on. Multiples of a number can be evenly divided by that number.

numerator the top number of a fraction. The numerator indicates the number of equal parts named.

obtuse angle an angle that is greater than 90° but less than 180°

obtuse triangle   a triangle having one obtuse angle

parallel lines   lines that are always the same distance apart

parallelogram   a quadrilateral in which opposite sides are parallel and equal in length

perimeter   the distance around a closed figure

perpendicular   meeting at right or 90° angles

plane figures   flat shapes that have only length and width, but no thickness. Circles, triangles, and squares are plane figures.

point   a dot or single location in space

polygon   a simple closed figure with three or more straight sides

probability   study of the likelihood or chances of an event occurring

product   the result in a multiplication problem. Example: In the number sentence $3 \times 4 = 12$, the product is 12.

proper fraction   a fraction in which the numerator is less than the denominator Example: $\frac{3}{5}$

proportion   an equation that shows equal ratios. Example: $\frac{3}{5} = \frac{6}{10}$

quadrilateral   a polygon with four sides. Rectangles and squares are quadrilaterals.

quotient   the result in a division problem. Example: In the number sentence $30 \div 6 = 5$, the quotient is 5.

radius   the distance from the center of a circle to the circumference

ratio   a comparison of two numbers. For example, 2 pounds for \$3 can be written as 2 to 3, 2 : 3, or $\frac{2}{3}$.

ray   part of a straight line that extends in one direction from a point

remainder   the amount left over when one number cannot be evenly divided by another

right angle   an angle that measures 90°

scale   a number line on a measurement tool

scalene triangle   a triangle in which no sides are equal

similar   exactly the same shape but not necessarily the same size

simplify   divide the numerator and denominator of a fraction by the same number

solids   three-dimensional figures

sphere   a solid that looks like a ball or a globe. The points on the face of a sphere are all the same distance from its center.

square   a quadrilateral with four equal sides and four equal angles

three-dimensional   Objects that take up space because they have length, width, and height. Examples include cubes, rectangular prisms (boxes), cones, pyramids, cylinders, and spheres.

trapezoid   a quadrilateral that has exactly one pair of parallel sides

triangle   a three-sided polygon

two-dimensional   shapes that can be drawn on paper or a flat surface. Shapes that have length and width but do not have thickness are two-dimensional. Examples include circles, triangles, squares, and ovals.

variable   a letter or symbol that represents one or more numbers. Example: In the expression $3 + n$, the variable n can represent many numbers.

vertex   the point where the sides of an angle, the sides of a polygon, or the edges of a solid meet

volume   the amount of space occupied by an object

Index